AI MEETS AGILE

TRANSFORMING THE WAY WE WORK

VINAY BABU TARALA

Vinay Babu Tarala
1st Edition

Publication Date: August 2025
Price: ₹ 499 / $ 11.99
ISBN: 978-93-7164-914-8
Published by:
Adhyyan Books
Office No. 589,
Opposite Vivanta by Taj,
DDA SFS. Pocket-1, Dwarka,
Sec-22, New Delhi-110077
Website: http://adhyyanbooks.com
E-mail: contact@adhyyanbooks.com

Printed at: Repro Printers, Delhi

DISCLAIMER

This publication is designed to provide information in regard to the subject matter covered. While every effort has been made to ensure accuracy and relevance, the author and publisher make no representations or warranties with respect to the completeness, applicability, or fitness of the contents of this work and disclaim any implied warranties.

The ideas, examples, case studies, and tools presented in this book are based on the author's professional experience, research, and interpretation of emerging trends in AI and Agile practices. Readers are advised to use discretion and professional judgment in applying any recommendations in their specific context.

The author and publisher shall not be held liable for any loss or damages arising directly or indirectly from the use of the information contained in this book.

Any references to companies, platforms, or products are for illustrative purposes only and do not imply endorsement. All trademarks and registered trademarks appearing in the book are the property of their respective owners.

This book is not intended as legal, financial, or professional advice. Readers should consult qualified professionals where appropriate.

CONTENTS

PREFACE

The world of work is undergoing a seismic shift. Artificial Intelligence is no longer a future concept—it's a present reality transforming how teams operate, products are built, and decisions are made. And yet, in the midst of this disruption, one principle remains timeless: agility.

This book was born at the intersection of two profound forces—AI and Agile. Over the years, I've had the privilege of leading digital transformation initiatives across global enterprises, helping organizations navigate the uncertainties of scale, speed, and complexity. In that journey, I witnessed firsthand the tension between experimentation and structure, innovation and governance, automation and empathy.

"AI Meets Agile: Transforming the Way We Work" is my response to that tension. It offers a blueprint, not just for surviving the AI era, but for thriving in it—with agility as the compass. Each chapter explores a practical aspect of integrating AI into Agile ways of working—from ceremonies and tooling to mindset, maturity, and leadership.

This book is for Agile practitioners seeking new tools, for leaders managing transformation, and for technologists curious about what's next. But more than that, it's for anyone who believes that technology is most powerful when it elevates human potential.

Thank you for taking the time to explore these ideas. I hope this book inspires new conversations, deeper experiments, and a shared commitment to building a more adaptive, inclusive, and intelligent future of work.

— Vinay Babu Tarala

ACKNOWLEDGMENTS

Thanks to my parents, **Tarala Saibaba** and **Tarala Balamani**, for raising me with the values of honesty, integrity, and ethical living.

Thanks to my beautiful wife, **Sandhya Rani**, who has been the backbone of my journey for the past nine years—constantly supporting me and surrounding me with unwavering positivity.

Thanks to my sisters, **Aruna** and **Thejaswi**, for their love and encouragement.

Thanks to my best friend, **Manohar Yerraguntla**, President of PMI Pearl City Hyderabad Chapter, for always pushing me to grow professionally—be it through becoming a subject matter expert, researching, or speaking at conferences.

Thanks to my guru, **Dr. Koti Reddy Bhavanam**, who truly transformed my life.

Thanks to my fellow friends from **PMIPCC**, my mentor **Venkat Reddy** and **Komal Mathur** for their belief in me.

Thanks to all my former colleagues at **Collins Aerospace**, especially **Vamsi Krishna Susarla** and **Kalyan Tiru-**

malashetty, who shaped my early professional path, and to those I worked with at **Optum Global Solutions**, **Union Bank of Switzerland**, and **Infosys Consulting** for enriching my journey.

Thanks to all fellow agile coaches—**Venkata Satish Kolla**, **Ashutosh Bhatawadekar**, **Sharath Adsumillie**, **Sunand Sharma**, **Deepthi Jain**, and others—for the learnings!

Thanks also to my former colleagues from my **Reckitt** journey, especially **Sree Nallagatla** and **Santhana Selvan**, for their partnership, resilience, and collaboration during pivotal transformation initiatives.

Thanks to my current organization **AT&T**, for the opportunity to explore and implement Agile and AI at scale and solve some of the most complex real-world problems.

Special thanks to my co-learners and fellow explorers in this journey who helped me shape my understanding through conversations, conflicts, collaborations, and courage.

AUTHOR'S NOTE

A 20-Year Dream. A 10-Year Chase. A 6-Month Sprint. And Now… 15 Chapters of Purpose.

Twenty years ago, as an engineering student, I had a dream—to write a book. I didn't know the title. I didn't know the genre. I just knew I wanted to build something that would last.

Ten years back, I came close. I thought I'd write about my Agile journey. I had stories. I had scars. But life had other plans—and the manuscript stayed a dream.

Then came the last five years—where my work as an Agile Coach collided with something powerful: the rise of AI. That's when I knew—this is the story I had to tell.

On January 1st this year, I announced my commitment:

Write and release "AI Meets Agile: Transforming the Way We Work" within six months.

This book is more than just a professional achievement—it's a personal milestone. It represents the intersection of curiosity and commitment, of learning and leading. Every chapter has been shaped by real-world experiences—by the Agile transformations I've led, by the AI tools I've explored, and by the people who've shared this journey with me.

The result is a book that blends frameworks and philosophy, strategy and soul. Whether you're an Agile practitioner, a tech leader, a product owner, or simply someone curious about the future of work—this book is for you.

Because AI doesn't replace us. When paired with empathy, agility, and purpose—it elevates us.

Thank you for being a part of this journey.

— Vinay Babu Tarala

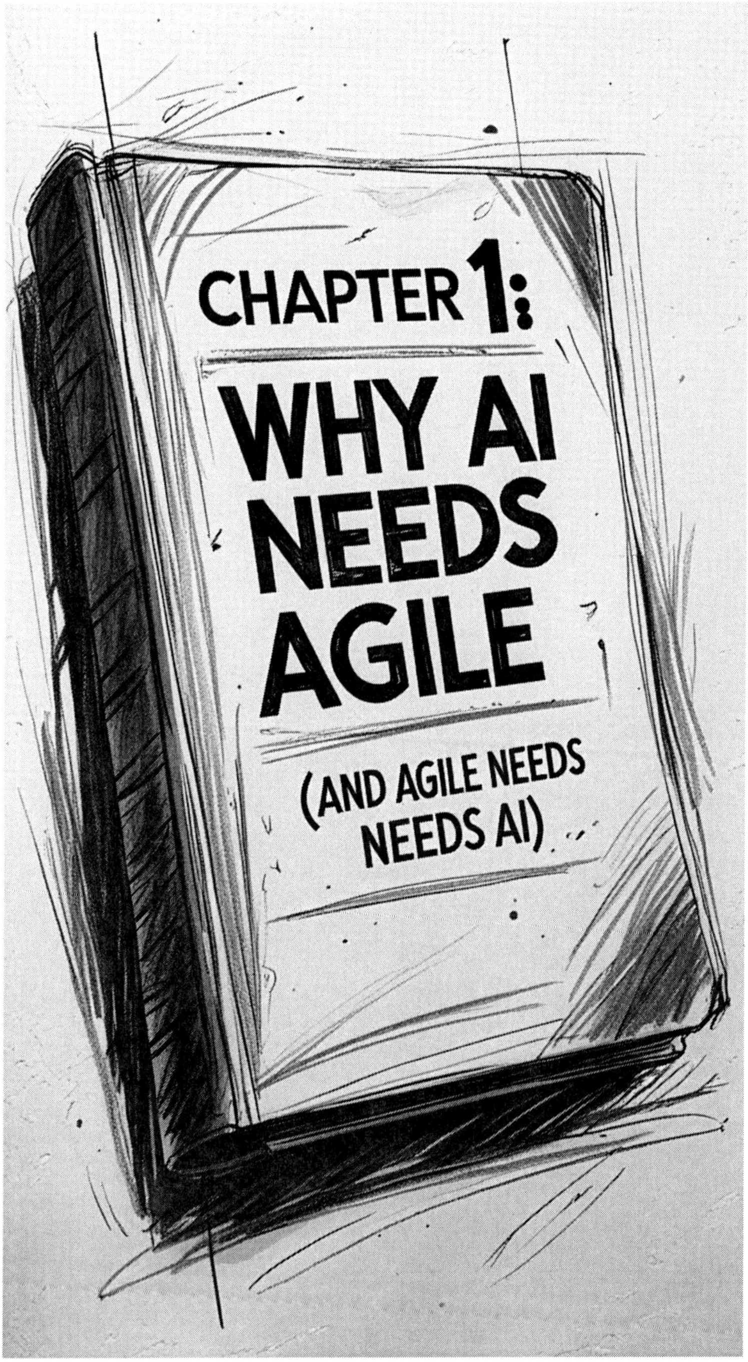
CHAPTER 1:
WHY AI NEEDS AGILE
(AND AGILE NEEDS
NEEDS AI)

1

WHY AI NEEDS AGILE (AND AGILE NEEDS AI)

THE NEW CONVERGENCE: AI MEETS AGILE

In the busy headquarters of an international financial institution in the spring of 2024, there were two groups on different sides of the same floor. One was working on an AI-based fraud detection tool employing the old-school (traditional) waterfall approach; carefully planning every stage, writing down each requirement, and having a schedule that looked 18 months into the future. The second team was developing an AI-powered customer service platform based on Agile methodologies, working two-week sprints, receiving constant feedback, and adjusting their method with every iteration.

Six months down the line, the waterfall team continued to hone requirements while their competitors released equivalent solutions. The Agile team, in contrast, had already had three iterations of their platform out into the world, each smarter and more responsive than its predecessor, winning crucial market share and customer learnings.

This story of two paths explains why AI and Agile are coming together now, during this critical juncture in technological development. With its hyperconnected, data-rich business environment, today's organizations are confronted with a dual challenge: unlocking the transformative potential of artificial intelligence while continuing to deliver speed, flexibility, and humanity if they are to remain competitive.

Artificial intelligence introduces unheard-of computational power, pattern detection, and automation. Agile gives you the design, attitude, and practices to control complexity and change. When combined, they achieve a tremendous synergy that empowers organizations to innovate quicker, make better decisions, and create more robust, future-proofed teams.

Why This Convergence Now?

The intersection of AI and Agile is not an accident; multiple powerful forces are transforming the way we work, innovate, and create value:

Speed of Innovation: Keeping Up with AI's Accelerating Evolution

AI technologies are changing at a rate that established delivery models just can't keep up with. Think about it: GPT-4 arrived only 15 months after GPT-3.5, but brought about a quantum change in capabilities. Companies employing traditional waterfall methodologies always find themselves at a disadvantage, strategizing around AI capabilities that grow obsolete before any implementation can be started.

Agile's iterative, incremental process enables teams to:

- Release minimum viable AI functionality early
- Get real-world feedback
- Integrate the newest algorithmic enhancements in every sprint
- Get ahead of rivals still stuck in extended planning cycles

Real Example: Netflix deploys two-week sprints to continuously optimize its recommendation algorithms, enabling them to roll in new AI techniques while still providing seamless user experience; a value proposition worth billions in customer loyalty.

Explosion of Data: Making Sense of the Information Deluge

We now create more data in one day than was created in all of history's previous centuries. The IDC estimates by 2025, the datasphere will be 175 zettabytes big, a number so enormous it boggles the mind.

Inside this sea of information are precious patterns, insights, and opportunities; if we can get to the bottom of them. AI is good at identifying signals in this noise, and Agile gives us the structure to:

- Iteratively experiment and test data hypotheses
- Construct incrementally more superior data pipelines and models
- Pivot rapidly when data shows up with surprise patterns
- Ship value even when operating on incomplete data

Real Example: Spotify's Discover Weekly playlist employs machine learning to analyse billions of data points regarding listening behaviour. Through working in Agile sprints, their data scientists continually tighten these recommendations, testing out new features while monitoring their influence on user engagement.

Uncertainty and Complexity: Operating in the Unpredictable

AI development and contemporary business contexts both feature high levels of uncertainty and complexity. AI projects are frequently about venturing into unexplored technical space, while businesses deal with unstable markets, changing regulations, and unpredictable competitive challenges.

- Agile was conceived exactly to handle such uncertainty:
- Working in the face of changing requirements instead of locking in rigid plans
- Prioritizing responsiveness over predictability
- Seeing working solutions as valuable assets rather than stoutly defending exhaustive documentation

- Pursuing customer collaboration ahead of negotiating contracts

AI supplements this strategy by:

- Giving insights that minimize uncertainty
- Pinpointing patterns humans may overlook
- Enabling frequent, automatic decisions to clear mental capacity
- Allowing quicker, data-driven course corrections

Real Example: Moderna applied Agile strategies paired with AI to create its COVID-19 vaccine within 42 days; a process that would normally take years. Their iterative strategy permitted them to realign as new knowledge emerged and AI sped up protein analysis and clinical trial design.

Demand for Personalization and Responsiveness: Embracing Increasing Expectations

Customers today demand personalized experiences and immediate responsiveness; responses that can only be achieved through the synergy of AI's personalization and Agile's customer focus.

AI provides the personalization in the form of:

- Individual user profiling and segmentation
- Adaptation in real-time to behaviours and preferences
- Predictive insights into future needs

- Natural language interfaces with a human touch

Agile makes this personalization adapt based on customer feedback through:

- Regular user testing and validation
- Customer-impact-based prioritization
- Faster integration of feedback
- Ongoing delivery of enhancements

Real Example: Duolingo utilizes AI to tailor language learning pathways for millions of learners, while utilizing Agile methodologies to pilot new capabilities with small segments of users prior to broader release. It has enabled them to deliver 80% higher completion rates than with traditional methods of language learning.

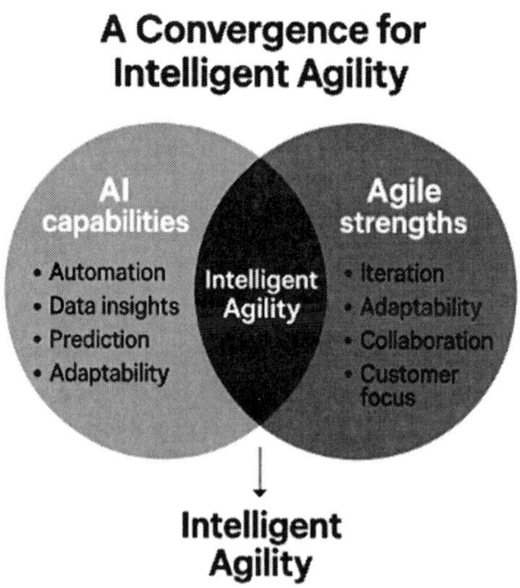

How AI Empowers Agile

While Agile has transformed software development over the past two decades, AI is now supercharging these practices across every phase of execution:

Backlog Management: From Gut Feel to Data-Driven Prioritization

Traditional backlog prioritization often relies heavily on stakeholder opinions and team intuition. AI transforms this process by:

- Analysing historical impact of similar features
- Processing customer feedback at scale to identify patterns
- Calculating risk factors and dependencies
- Recommending best order by business value, effort, and technical risk

The product owner still gets the final say, but now with data-driven guidance that enhances human decision-making.

Tool example: ProductBoard and Aha! now include AI capabilities that analyze customer feedback across channels, group like requests, and recommend priority levels based on business value and strategic fit.

Sprint Planning: Smart Workload Allocation

AI adds intelligence to capacity planning and work allocation through:

- Task sizing suggestions from analogous previous stories
- Load balancing the team for skills and availability
- Velocity-based forecasting capacity, factoring in historical velocity and team change
- Identification of likely bottlenecks and dependencies early on

This frees Scrum Masters and teams from petty negotiating about points and assignments and enables them to spend their time on more valuable conversations.

Tool example: Azure DevOps now has AI-facilitated sprint planning tools that provide story point estimate suggestions based on description complexity and past team performance.

Daily Stand-ups: From Status Reports to Trend Identification

NLP-powered assistants are turning daily stand-ups into information-producing sessions from run-of-the-mill updates:

- Automatically extracting the gist of team discussions
- Identifying repeated blockers requiring escalation
- Monitoring progress trends over sprints
- Creating follow-up tasks out of commitments made

It changes the focus from "what did you do yesterday?" to "what patterns are emerging in our work?"

Tool example: ScrumGenius and Standuply employ AI to generate pre-meeting summaries, record action items, and flag discussion topics to explore further, shortening stand-ups to 7 minutes on average from 15 minutes.

Retrospectives: Sentiment-Aware Continuous Improvement

Emotional intelligence is brought to team retrospectives by AI through:

- Analysis of team discussion sentiment to reveal underlying issues
- Recognition of patterns across several retros to highlight chronic issues
- Proposing improvement experiments based on high-performing teams
- Monitoring of action item follow-through and effectiveness

This enables teams to go from debating on the surface to also solving root causes of performance problems.

Tool Example: TeamRetro and EasyRetro now offer AI functionality that reviews transcripts of meetings, identifies emotional trends, and recommends topics for discussion based on team interaction.

Velocity Forecasting: From Guesswork to Prediction

Legacy velocity calculations are typically lagging averages. AI facilitates predictive analytics that:

- Make statistical predictions of likely completion ranges with confidence intervals
- Account for changes in team composition, holidays, and outside dependencies
- Recognize early warning signs of technical debt or scope creep
- Suggest scope adjustments from actual progress in real-time

This enables teams to respond proactively instead of reactively to delivery risks.

Tool Example: Jira's road mapping capabilities now incorporate machine learning models that calculate completion dates with confidence intervals, allowing teams to communicate realistic schedules to stakeholders.

How Agile Makes AI Better

While AI fuels Agile practices, the same is also true in reverse. Agile methodologies are the ideal setup for viable AI projects:

Iterative Delivery: Critical to AI Experimentation

AI development does not take a straight line from idea to finish. It involves investigation, experimentation, and repeated reassessment. Agile's iterative nature allows for:

- Fast testing of model hypotheses

- Incremental accuracy and performance upgrades
- Early detection of data quality flaws
- Regular integration of new training data

This avoids the "big bang" method that causes most AI initiatives to end up in failure after months of unseen effort.

Real-world example: JPMorgan Chase's Contract Intelligence (COiN) platform, used to extract information from contracts, was built iteratively across several sprints. Accuracy was enhanced by a few percentage points per sprint until it achieved human-level quality while providing business value at every milestone.

Fail-Fast Learning: Pivoting When Models Underperform

Not every AI method will work. Agile's focus on early feedback enables teams to:

- Identify immediately when a model is not doing as predicted
- Pivot into different methods without sunk cost fallacy
- Learn from errors and not conceal them
- Keep stakeholder confidence by being open

This way turns "failed" AI projects into good learning experiences that inform ultimate success.

Real-world example: Amazon's recommendation algorithm improved over several cycles, with the team discarding several promising strategies that failed to yield in real-life testing. Every "failure" led to the next sprint's strategy, eventually developing into one of the most lucrative AI systems in retail history.

Cross-Functional Collaboration: Bridging Disciplines AI endeavours demand variety of skill; data scientists, engineers, domain specialists, ethicists, and business stakeholders. Agile practice enables this collaboration through:

- Cross-functional teams with common goals
- Daily synchronization to keep everyone in sync
- Sprint reviews that bring multiple points of view
- Shared ownership of results, not siloed responsibilities

This keeps the all-too-familiar gap between data science research and applied implementation at bay.

Real-world example: Wayfair assembled cross-functional "pod" teams of data scientists, engineers, designers, and merchandising professionals to build their visual search feature. With two-week sprints, these multifaceted teams delivered a solution that enhanced the technical precision and business salience of search results.

Ethical Checks: Creating Responsible AI

With increasing influence over critical choices, ethical thinking must take priority. Ceremonies of Agile naturally serve as points of ethical review:

- Defining user stories can incorporate fairness criteria
- Sprint planning can dedicate time to bias testing

- Code reviews can analyse algorithmic transparency
- Retrospectives can consider unforeseen ethical impacts

This integrated method makes ethics an ongoing concern and not an afterthought.

Real-world example: Humana health insurance integrates "ethical user stories" into their AI development sprints so that every feature satisfies clear fairness requirements for various patient groups. This practice prevented them from adopting biases that could have harmed specific demographic groups.

Market Signals: It's Already Happening

The marriage of AI and Agile is not theoretical; it's already changing organizations across sectors:

Sequoia Capital, a top venture capital firm globally, released a 2023 report hailing AI as "the biggest opportunity since the internet" but cautioning that seizing this opportunity involves flexible, Agile teams in a position to iterate rapidly on AI-fueled solutions.

Deloitte's 2025 Human Capital Trends report shows that 70% of high-performing organizations are investing in integrated AI + Agile programs and that firms have achieved 2.3x higher rates of innovation when these capabilities are built together, not alone.

Google Cloud is integrating AI into each level of business infrastructure, while also embracing scaled Agile frameworks to assist their clients in deploying these capabilities. Internal research indicates that teams that implement Agile processes are 65% more likely to be able to successfully deploy AI models.

McKinsey's Global Survey reveals that organizations using Agile practices along with AI projects are 3 times as likely to realize ROI in the first year compared to those applying conventional project management for AI deployment.

A Tale of Two Transformations

Imagine two banks undertaking AI-driven customer service projects:

Bank A takes a classical route. They spend six months of requirements gathering, develop exhaustive specifications for an AI chatbot, and schedule a one-year development phase before implementation. By the time they go live, customer expectations have changed, competitors have come out with better solutions, and the underlying AI technology has made leaps of progress beyond their specs. Their chatbot looks stale upon implementation and does not deliver business goals.

Bank B adopts an Agile mindset. They begin with a basic chatbot servicing elementary questions and roll it out to a limited customer base in six weeks' time. They collect usage metrics, determine the top-value intents, and incrementally add capabilities to the model every two weeks. They continually add the newest NLP innovation and pivot to new customer requirements as they arise. In six months, they have a market-leading solution that closely maps customer needs.

The difference isn't resources or talent; it's approach. Bank B's combination of Agile methodology with AI technology allowed them to learn and adapt faster than their competitor.

The Organizational Impact

The convergence of AI and Agile isn't just changing how we build technology, it's transforming organizational structures and roles:

- Product Owners need data literacy to understand AI capabilities and limitations
- Scrum Masters facilitate collaboration between technical and domain experts
- Developers collaborate with data scientists in combined teams
- QA experts build new capabilities for testing probabilistic systems
- Stakeholders are trained to comment on model outputs instead of features only

Organizations that acknowledge and embrace these new roles will be well suited to realize the benefit of AI using Agile delivery.

Key Takeaways

- As we finish this chapter and move on to discuss particular frameworks in detail beyond Scrum, keep these key points in mind:
- AI and Agile are complementary forces; AI brings the intelligent capabilities, and Agile brings the delivery framework to apply them effectively.
- Agile provides AI projects with the structure they require to succeed; avoiding the usual pitfalls of overly ambitious scope, poor stakeholder alignment, and inability to deliver business value.
- AI accelerates Agile teams to be faster, smarter, and more insight-driven, enabling human judgment to be supported by data-fuelled intelligence at each step of the journey.
- The moment to embed them is today, companies that delay will be trying to play catch-up in a market where AI + Agile is the new baseline for competitiveness.

Later, in the next chapter, we will shift beyond Scrum and look at how other Agile frameworks: Kanban, SAFe, and Lean, are adapting to enable AI projects across varied scales and organizational contexts.

Chapter 2: Beyond Scrum - Smarter Ways to be Agile

2

BEYOND SCRUM

SMARTER WAYS TO BE AGILE

INTRODUCTION: THE AGILE FRAMEWORK ECOSYSTEM

When most folks hear "Agile," they instantly think of Scrum; two-week iterations, stand-up meetings every day, story points, and burndown charts. It's no wonder: Scrum is by far the most widespread implementation of Agile values and principles in thousands of organizations across the globe. However, Scrum is only one interpretation of the values and principles of the Agile Manifesto, tuned to a particular kind of work and team shapes.

As artificial intelligence transforms the way we work, make decisions, and create value, it's increasingly obvious that the default Scrum approach won't always be the most suitable for AI-based projects. The peculiarities of AI development; from data preparation and model training through experimentation and ongoing retraining; usually require different approaches that have other cadences, workflows, and scaling modes.

In this chapter, we'll discuss how the other Agile frameworks; Kanban, SAFe (Scaled Agile Framework), and Lean; can serve as superior foundations for particular kinds of AI work. We'll look at their fundamental principles, how they supplement AI development cycles, and when to implement each framework for your individual context and objectives.

Why Look Beyond Scrum

Scrum has a popularity for a reason. It delivers distinct roles, ceremonies, and artifacts that enable small, collocated teams to deliver incremental value in iterative cycles. For most product development contexts, particularly when developing customer-visible-facing features with clearly defined requirements, Scrum is a wonderful structure.

But AI projects bring a special set of challenges that can stretch the Scrum structure to its limits:

Data Infrastructure at Scale

AI projects tend to rely on huge data infrastructure that touches across many systems, necessitates domain-specialized skills, and includes long-lived processes. An average machine learning pipeline may involve:

- Gathering data from various sources
- Cleaning and preprocessing processes
- Feature engineering and data transformation

- Model training on clusters of distributed computing
- Validation on many datasets
- Deployment on edge devices or cloud providers

These tasks don't always neatly divide into sprint-sized amounts with clear expectations at the end of every cycle.

Research and Experimentation

In contrast to conventional software development in which solutions are written according to established method, AI development will frequently require large amounts of research and experimentation:

- Experimenting with several algorithms on the same problem
- Hyperparameter tuning by way of thousands of iterations
- Trying new methods when established ones fail
- Fixing unusual behaviour in trained models

This experimental process is what makes teams spend weeks down a path that never will work; a state of affairs that contradicts Scrum's requirement for tangible progress on every sprint.

Cross-Functional and Distributed Expertise

AI teams usually need a larger set of specialized capabilities than usual software teams:

- Data scientists for model development

- Data engineers for building pipelines
- Domain experts for selecting features
- Software engineers for integrating systems
- Ethics specialists for ethical AI implementation

Piling all of these capabilities in one tight, collocated team is becoming harder to find, particularly with worldwide competition for AI talent. This frequently requires distributed teams with centers of excellence; a configuration that Scrum wasn't really built to handle.

Enterprise-Wide Value Streams

Most of the transformational AI projects across multiple departments or value streams:

- A recommendation engine brushing up against marketing, product, and customer service
- A forecasting system impacting finance, supply chain, and operations
- A customer intelligence platform employed by sales, support, and product teams

These cross-cutting concerns demand coordination that exceeds what a single Scrum team can deliver, coupled with governance structures to guarantee consistent methods of data use, model creation, and ethical issues.

Considering these challenges, it's valid to consider other Agile frameworks that may better suit the special needs of AI development. Let's discuss each in turn.

1. Kanban + AI: Flow Meets Insight

Kanban originated in Toyota's production system but has been widely applied in knowledge work by its focus on visualizing the workflow, capping work in progress, and optimizing the flow. These principles make it very suitable for AI model development, experimentation, and operations (MLOps).

Core Principles of Kanban

Kanban is founded on a number of core principles:

- Visualize the workflow: Visualize the work by making things visible on a board using cards that flow through specified states
- Limit work in progress (WIP): Minimize multitasking to maximize flow and quality
- Manage flow: Maximize smooth movement of work items over individual utilization
- Make policies explicit: Make sure everyone knows how work flows through the system
- Implement feedback loops: Frequent reviews to enhance the process
- Improve collaboratively: Evolutionary improvement based on collective understanding

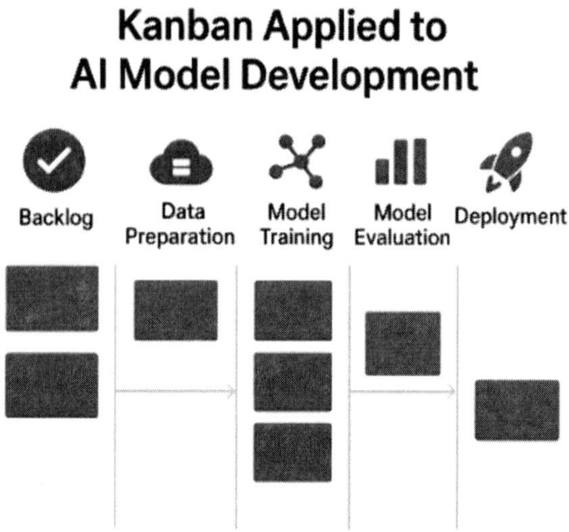

How Kanban Accelerates AI Development

The adaptive, flow-centric approach of Kanban has a number of benefits for AI teams:

Visualizing the Complex AI Lifecycle

AI development is many phases with much to gain from explicit visualization:

- Data gathering and preparation
- Feature engineering
- Model selection and training
- Hyperparameter tuning
- Validation and testing
- Deployment and monitoring
- Retraining and improvement

Kanban effectively makes these phases salient, indicating where work items are in the flow and where bottlenecks are occurring.

Dealing with Unpredictable Research Work

Unlike software development where task estimation has been quite mature, AI research work is frequently truly unpredictable. Kanban fits that reality by:

- Highlighting flow over dedicated-length sprints
- Enabling work items to take as long as they need to be finished
- Stressing limiting WIP to keep from having too many experiments in parallel
- Giving clear visibility into what's actually occurring, not what was intended to happen

Real-World Example: Microsoft Research AI

Microsoft Research AI implemented a Kanban system, but with adjustments, with their natural language processing team. They have dedicated columns for data preparation, model experimentation, evaluation, and publication on their board. Instead of imposing artificial sprint boundaries, they employ WIP limits to keep it focused while researching threads take their normal development time. This resulted in 40% more successful model deployments than their earlier sprint-based system.

Kanban Tools for AI Teams

A number of tools have arisen to enable Kanban workflows for AI development:

- ZenHub + GitHub: Combines Kanban boards with code repositories and MLOps pipelines
- Azure DevOps Boards: Has support for custom columns for AI-specific phases with native analytics
- Jira + Advanced Roadmaps: Supports hierarchical Kanban boards that can manage both high-level AI initiatives and granular tasks
- Trello + Power-Ups: Offers basic Kanban boards with add-ons for monitoring model metrics

The solution is to set these tools up to report on AI-specific metrics such as model accuracy, data readiness, and inference performance in addition to classical flow metrics.

2. SAFe + AI: Scaling Intelligence Across the Enterprise

Where Kanban is strong on team-level flow optimization, most AI projects need alignment with enterprise strategy and coordination across multiple teams. The Scaled Agile Framework (SAFe) offers an end-to-end methodology for scaling Agile practices in large organizations; making it highly useful for enterprise-wide AI transformation.

Core Principles of SAFe

SAFe is based on a number of core principles:

- Take an economic view: Create the best value and quality with the least investment
- Use systems thinking: Improve the entire system, not pieces
- Presume variability; retain options: Keep several alternatives before committing
- Develop incrementally with rapid, integrated learning cycles: Produce small lots for quick feedback
- Use objective evaluation to set milestones: Utilize working systems to provide evidence of progress
- Visualize and restrict WIP, decrease batch sizes, control queue lengths: Optimize flow throughout
- Use cadence, harmonize with cross-domain planning: Establish predictability and contain uncertainty
- Unleash the inherent motivation of knowledge workers: Engage autonomy, mastery, and purpose
- Decentralize decision-making: Facilitate quicker decisions near the work

How SAFe Improves Enterprise AI Initiatives

SAFe's framework for scaling Agile offers a number of advantages for organizations rolling out AI across teams and functions:

- Coordinating AI Strategy Through Portfolio Management
- SAFe's portfolio level enables organizations to:
- Align AI initiatives with strategic business goals

- Allocate money to high-priority AI opportunities
- Set up governance for responsible AI development
- Balance exploration (new AI abilities) with exploitation (utilizing tried approaches)

Synchronizing AI Development With Agile Release Trains

SAFe's program layer aligns teams into Agile Release Trains (ARTs); teams of 5-12 that work collaboratively on a common mission. It is perfect for sophisticated AI initiatives:

- A specialized Data & AI ART can deliver bespoke capabilities throughout the enterprise
- Multiple ARTs can align AI feature development with platform capabilities
- Program Increment (PI) planning enforces cross-team synchronization every 8-12 weeks
- System demos highlight integrated AI capabilities instead of disparate parts

Example: Capital One

Capital One structured its machine learning capacity in a separate AI/ML Agile Release Train that serves multiple product-centric ARTs. This alignment enables domain-specialized data scientists to keep centers of excellence yet remain integrated with customer-facing features. At PI Planning time, AI capabilities are aligned with product requirements, building a roadmap of harmonized deliveries. This strategy enabled Capital One to cut fraud by more than $100 million while also enhancing customer experience.

SAFe Tools for AI Governance

A number of tools facilitate SAFe application for AI projects:

- Jira Align: Offers portfolio-to-team visibility of AI investments
- Digital.ai (previously CollabNet VersionOne): Includes integrated support for SAFe artifacts and ceremonies
- Targetprocess: Facilitates AI capabilities visualization for teams and ARTs
- Microsoft Azure DevOps + SAFe templates: Merges development tools with SAFe framework

3. Lean + AI: Cutting Waste with Smarts

Whereas Kanban and SAFe offer process models, Lean thinking provides a supporting philosophy emphasizing the maximization of customer value and the elimination of waste. It is a philosophical complement that complements AI's strengths in pattern detection, process optimization, and automatic decision-making.

Core Principles of Lean

Lean is founded upon several essential principles:

- Define value from the customer's point of view: Prioritize what matters to users

- Map the value stream: Map out all steps in the delivery of value
- Create flow: Smooth movement without waiting lines
- Establish pull: Make only what is needed, and not forecasts
- Pursue perfection: Refine processes consistently

How Lean Improves AI Development and Operations

Lean emphasis on eliminating waste and ongoing improvement creates a strong foundation for AI projects:

- Determining Value and Waste in AI Processes
- Lean thinking allows AI teams to differentiate between:
- Value-adding activities (model construction that addresses real customer issues)
- Required non-value activities (data preparation, documentation)
- Pure waste (rebuilding models with no real improvements, gathering unused data)

This clarity allows teams to concentrate AI efforts on what's most important.

Elevating Lean Metrics with AI

AI has the potential to turbocharge standard Lean metrics and analyses:

- Lead Time Prediction: Machine learning models are able to predict finish times from historical trends and present work characteristics
- Root Cause Analysis: AI can detect relationships and possible causes in sophisticated systems that human analysis may overlook
- Defect Prediction: Models can indicate probable quality flaws before they happen
- Value Stream Optimization: Simulation and reinforcement learning can propose process enhancements

Real-World Example: Toyota Connected

Toyota Connected uses Lean AI strategies in their connected car offerings. Their staff leverage machine learning to examine telemetrics data from cars, looking for patterns that suggest quality problems or the need for maintenance. These data points are then used in ongoing improvement loops, with AI providing recommendations for process changes that human subject matter experts review and apply. Blending AI-driven analysis and Lean philosophy decreased warranty claims by 18% while enhancing customer satisfaction ratings.

Lean AI Tools

A number of tools facilitate Lean AI adoption:

- Celonis Process Mining + ML: Automatically identifies and examines processes, then recommends optimizations

- IBM Operational Decision Manager: Integrates business rules with machine learning for more intelligent decisions
- Signavio Process Intelligence: Maps value streams and uses AI to recognize improvement opportunities
- Tableau + Einstein Analytics: Visualizes the flow of value and recognizes waste through patterns

4. Selecting the Right Framework for AI Work

With several viable frameworks, how do you select the appropriate approach for your AI efforts? The response will vary with your team context, organizational type, and character of your AI work.

Framework Selection Criteria

- Keep these items in mind when choosing an Agile framework for AI development:
- Team Size and Distribution
- Small, co-located teams: Scrum or Kanban
- Multiple teams in a department: Kanban or SAFe Essential
- Enterprise-wide efforts: SAFe Large Solution or Portfolio

AI Work Characteristics

- Research-intensive, experimental: Kanban
- Product-centric AI capabilities: Scrum
- AI-driven process optimization: Lean

- Enterprise-level AI platform: SAFe

Organizational Objectives

- Speed to market: Scrum or Kanban
- Value stream coordination: SAFe
- Waste elimination and efficiency: Lean
- Innovation and exploration: Kanban

Framework Comparison Matrix

Framework Comparison Matrix

Aspect	Scrum	Kanban	Safe	Lean
Best For	Product teams	Research/ML	Enterprises	Ops/Process
Team Size	Small (5-9)	Flexible	Multiple teams	Flexible
Planning Cadence	Fixed sprints	Continuous	Multi-level	Flow-based
Change Process	Between sprints	Anytime	Coordinated	Continuous
Metrics Focus	Velocity	Flow efficiency	Predictability	Value/waste ratio
AI Advantage	Quick feedback on features	Flexible tracking of experiments	Scaled coordination	Intelligent automation & waste reduction

Hybrid Methodologies

Most organizations find that hybrid methodologies best apply to AI projects:

- Scrum + Kanban (Scrumban): Sprint organization with flow-driven work management within sprints

- SAFe + Lean: Enterprise alignment with removal of waste emphasis
- Kanban + Lean: Optimization of flow with ongoing improvement

The secret is to fit the framework to your context and not to try to make your context fit the framework.

Real-World Example: Hybrid AI Framework at Spotify

Spotify's well-known "Squad" approach illustrates how hybrid frameworks can enable AI at scale. Their process integrates:

- Scrum for feature teams developing customer-facing AI functionality
- Kanban for data science and research teams investigating new algorithms
- Lean for ongoing improvement of data pipelines and infrastructure
- Tribe and Chapter organization (like SAFe ARTs and Communities of Practice) for cross-cutting issues

This hybrid approach enables them to have both autonomy at the squad level and alignment within their organization, speeding their delivery of AI-driven music discovery features while continuously refining their recommendation algorithms.

Key Takeaways

As we finish exploring Agile frameworks outside of Scrum, keep these key takeaways in mind:

- There's no single solution to AI + Agile integration. Various frameworks have different purposes, and the best one for you is contingent on your unique situation.
- Bore beyond Scrum for the frameworks that are more experimentally suitable, scalable, and enterprise-capable. Kanban, SAFe, and Lean have some useful alternatives or complements to pure Scrum.
- The best framework match is based on your team's objectives, makeup, and type of AI work. Use team size, work type, and organizational objectives to inform your choice.
- Hybrid methodologies tend to be best suited to intricate AI projects. Don't hesitate to take pieces of various methodologies and merge them into a tailored approach.

In the following chapter, we'll discuss how AI is revolutionizing conventional Agile roles, adding new features such as copilots and autonomous agents that fundamentally alter how Agile teams work and interact with each other.

Chapter 3:
Meet Your AI Teammate —
The Agile Teammat -
Agille Copilot
The Agile Copilot

3

MEET YOUR AI TEAMMATE

THE AGILE COPILOT

INTRODUCTION: THE DAWN OF DIGITAL COLLABORATION

Imagine walking into your team's daily stand-up and getting a personalized brief from your AI colleague: "Based on yesterday's commits and Slack conversations, Jake seems stuck on the authentication module. Sarah's testing pipeline discovered three edge cases that might affect the sprint goal. The customer feedback from last week's demo suggests we should prioritize the mobile responsiveness story. This isn't science fiction; it's the reality of AI-augmented Agile teams in 2025." This is not science fiction.

A new class of digital collaborators; AI copilots and autonomous agents; is emerging as artificial intelligence becomes a fundamental facilitator of Agile transformation. These intelligent systems are joining rather than replacing human team members as specialized colleagues with special skills. They are quite good at managing routine chores that liberate brain space for higher-value activities, seeing trends people would overlook, and processing enormous volumes of data.

Including artificial intelligence copilots into Agile teams marks a basic change in our conception of teamwork. We are dealing with digital entities that can learn, adapt, and significantly contribute to team outcomes, not only with technologies to assist our work. This chapter looks at how these artificial intelligence colleagues are changing each Agile function, their limitations, and how best to include them into the DNA of your team.

What is an AI Copilot?

An artificial intelligence copilot differs essentially from conventional software tools. Conventional tools wait for particular inputs to generate predefined outputs; artificial intelligence copilots actively participate in processes, learn from context, and proactively propose enhancements. They mark a new paradigm in human-computer interaction, one in which the computer transforms from a passive tool to a cooperative partner.

Main Attributes of AI Copilots

Agile environments allow artificial intelligence copilots to share numerous key traits:

- **Contextual Awareness**: By means of constant data analysis from several sources; sprint boards,

code repositories, communication channels, and user feedback platforms, they grasp the present situation of projects, team dynamics, and business priorities.
- **Proactive Intelligence**: Rather than waiting for questions, proactive intelligence surfaces ideas, points out hazards, and recommends improvements based on trends in team performance and project data.
- **Natural Language Interface**: Since they speak in human language, any team members; technical or not; may access their insights.
- **Continuous Learning**: They keep learning by seeing results and including team member comments, thereby refining their suggestions over time.
- **Multi-Modal Integration**: Working across several platforms and tools, multi-modal integration creates a consistent intelligence layer across the whole Agile toolchain.

The Stack of Technology Supporting AI Copilots

Modern artificial intelligence copilots on three fundamental technologies:

- Natural language processing (NLP) helps to interpret and generate human language for analysis of textual content including user tales, comments, and feedback as well as for documentation and communication.

- Powers forecasting skills, pattern identification, and intelligent suggestions depending on past data and present trends by use of machine learning and predictive analytics.
- Processes visual data from diagrams, wireframes, and user interface mock-ups to grasp design intent and recommend enhancements in computer vision.
- Connect with current Agile tools and platforms to access data and automate activities all throughout the development environment.
- Real-time data processing lets instantaneous analysis of streaming data from many sources produce accurate insights and alarms.

Common AI Copilot Systems

Leaders in the AI copilot scene have come out from several platforms:

- Originally concentrating on code generation, GitHub Copilot is now covering code review support, test case development, and documentation production.
- Joined across Jira, Confluence, and other Atlassian technologies, Atlassian Intelligence offers smart summaries, automated processes, and intelligent content creation.
- Embedded in Azure DevOps and GitHub, Microsoft Copilot for DevOps supports project planning, code analysis, and deployment optimization.

- Miro AI improves collaborative whiteboarding with intelligent content creation, template recommendations, and meeting facilitation.
- For today's modern development teams, linear artificial intelligence offers smart project insights, automated status updates, and intelligent issue tracking.

How AI Copilots Transform Agile Roles: Role-by- Role Augmentation

The effects of artificial intelligence copilots fluctuate greatly depending on the Agile roles; each position gains from specific AI capabilities catered to their particular tasks and challenges.

1. **Scrum Master**: The Orchestration Specialist

The Scrum Master job has always been one of removing obstacles and enabling team effectiveness. AI copilots provide hitherto unheard-of insight into team dynamics and process efficiency, therefore enhancing these skills.

Improved Capacity for Facilitation

Automated Meeting Preparation: By examining current behaviour across all team tools, AI copilots can pre-populate stand-up agendas. They pinpoint important subjects for conversation, possible roadblocks, and progress reports so Scrum Masters may concentrate on facilitation instead of data collecting.

Real-Time Pattern Recognition: AI may examine conversation patterns, participation levels, and sentiment in meetings to find when team members are disengaging or when sessions are turning unproductive. This lets Scrum Masters change their facilitation style right away.

Impediment Intelligence: AI copilots can proactively find developing constraints by tracking code repositories, support tickets, and team conversations, therefore giving Scrum Masters early warning to solve problems.

Real-World Example: Spotify's Obstacle Predictability

Using an artificial intelligence copilot to examine trends in their internal communication tools, code review cycles, and deployment data, Spotify's Agile teams Early indicators of technical debt accumulation or team coordination problems notify Scrum Masters with tailored advice. Over their engineering company, this proactive approach has cut the average obstruction resolving time by 45%.

Monitoring Mood and Engagement

Tracking team health metrics that are typically challenging to measure is one of the most useful skills artificial intelligence copilots bring to Scrum Masters.

Sentiment Analysis: AI can spot patterns in team morale, stress levels, and involvement by examining the tone and substance of team emails. This enables Scrum Masters to act before little problems grow to be significant concerns.

Participation Pattern Analysis: AI can monitor participation levels in meetings and asynchronous interactions, spotting team members who could be struggling, overburdled, or disinterested.

Workload Balance Monitoring: AI can assist Scrum Masters in determining whether team members are overburdened or underused by examining work distribution and completion patterns.

2. **Product Owner**: The Value Maximiser

Product owners must constantly prioritize features and maximize value delivery with little knowledge or time. By offering data-driven insights that complement human judgment, artificial intelligence copilots change this function.

Smart Backlog Control

Smart Prioritization: AI copilots can advise backlog prioritizing by analysing many data sources; customer feedback, usage analytics, company metrics, technical difficulty estimates. They consider things like the relationship between feature utilization and client retention that would be challenging for people to weigh concurrently.

Story Generation from Feedback: Natural language processing tools let artificial intelligence turn unstructured consumer comments into organized user stories with success criteria and acceptance criteria. This guarantees true user voice and drastically lessens the time Product Owners spend creating stories.

Influence Forecasting: AI copilots may forecast the expected influence of suggested features on important business indicators by means of previous data on related characteristics, therefore guiding Product Owners in their prioritizing decisions.

Real-World Example: AI-Driven Airbnb Product Discovery

Competitive Analysis: Using an artificial intelligence copilot to constantly examine user activity data, app store reviews, and customer support queries, Airbnb's Product Owners find developing demands and pain areas. The system creates hypothesis-driven feature requests automatically, including suggested success criteria and supporting data. This strategy has cut three weeks on average from idea to development while raising the success rate of new feature introductions by 38%.

Integration of market intelligence

Competitive Analysis: \AI copilots can track market trends, competitor activity, and product releases to enable Product Owners to grasp the competitive environment and spot chances for uniqueness.

Customer Sentiment Tracking: Through social media, review, and support contact analysis, artificial intelligence offers real-time insights into consumer satisfaction and points up developing trends in user needs.

ROI Projection: Machine learning models can project the possible return on investment for various feature choices, therefore guiding Product Owners in their strategic resource allocation.

3. **Developers & Testers**: The Technical Accelerators

AI copilots provide the most advanced and generally accepted tools for members of development teams, mostly targeted on expediting technical work while preserving quality.

Code Development Acceleration

Intelligent Code Generation: Tools like GitHub Copilot and Amazon CodeWhisperer can create code snippets, whole functions, and even whole modules depending on natural language descriptions or context from current code.

Code Review Assistance: AI may automatically find possible flaws, security vulnerabilities, and code quality problems during the review process so free (to free up)ing human reviewers to concentrate on design and business logic issues.

Documentation Automation: By examining code structure and comments, AI copilots may produce thorough documentation for code, APIs, and system designs.

Improving Tests

Automated Test Case Generation: Analysing code routes and business needs allows AI to provide thorough test cases including edge situations human testers would overlook.

Risk-Based Testing:AI may examine previous defect trends and code changes to find areas of most risk, therefore enabling teams to concentrate their testing activities where most needed.

Test Data Generation: By use of synthetic data production, artificial intelligence may produce realistic test datasets covering several scenarios, therefore safeguarding sensitive data.

Real-World Example: AI-Enhanced Development at Microsoft

AI copilots included into Visual Studio and GitHub used by Microsoft's development teams offer real-time recommendations for security updates, code enhancements, and performance optimizations. From the combined knowledge of Microsoft's development community, the system learns to offer contextually relevant recommendations. Teams utilizing these artificial intelligence copilots report 40% less security flaws in production code and 25% faster development cycles.

4. **Agile Coach**: The Team Optimization Specialist

Working across several teams, Agile Coaches enhance Agile methods and organizational agility. AI copilots give them scalable means to monitor transformation progress, evaluate team health, and spot areas for development.

Study of Team Dynamics

Communication Pattern Analysis: AI can examine communication flows both inside and between teams to spot any silos, cooperation bottlenecks, or excess of data.

Practice Maturity Assessment: AI can evaluate team performance and behaviours by means of practice maturity assessments, therefore guiding particular enhancements based on Agile practices' implementation by teams.

Cross-Team Learning: AI copilots can spot effective methods used in high-performance teams and suggest their implementation in teams dealing with comparable problems.

Support for Scaled Coaching

Personalized Coaching Recommendations: AI can provide focused coaching approaches and track their efficacy over time depending on team-specific issues and settings.

Transformation Metrics: AI may compile and examine data from several teams to offer insights into general transformation development and point up systemic problems.

Resource Optimization: Analysis of coaching demand and team needs enables artificial intelligence to help allocate coaching resources around the company.

Use Case Deep Dive: OpenAI Operator in Sprint Planning

Let's look at a thorough case study of how a finance firm included OpenAI's Operator (a fictional advanced AI agent) into their sprint planning process to show the pragmatic influence of AI copilots.

The Difficulties

Series B finance startup TechFin Solutions was having trouble with often running over time inefficient sprint planning sessions that produced badly balanced sprints. Their obstacles consisted in:

- Divergent story prioritizing among several Product Owners

- Task complexity estimation challenges with new technologies

- Limited insight of team member capabilities and competency

- Insufficient data-driven analysis of which features truly added value

The Integration of AI

The researchers combined an artificial intelligence copilot with these features:

Historical Analysis: The artificial intelligence examined two years of sprint data including customer feedback scores, defect rates, and story completion rates to spot trends in both successful and failed effort.

Real-Time Capacity Assessment: Monitoring code changes, pull request reviews, and calendar availability helped the AI keep a dynamic perspective of every team member's capacity and present workload.

Predictive Prioritization: Combining consumer usage data, support ticket trends, and business metric correlations, the algorithm suggested narrative prioritizing depending on potential impact.

The Implementation Process

Week 1-2: Data Integration To create complete data access, the team linked their AI copilot to Jira, GitHub, consumer support systems, and corporate intelligence dashboards.

Week 3-4: Calibration Period The team could calibrate its recommendations against known results when the AI system examined past data started offering recommendations alongside human decisions.

Week 5-8: Guided Implementation Among numerous inputs, sprint planning sessions featured AI recommendations; the team responded on the quality and applicability of ideas.

Week 9+: Full Integration Standardly present in sprint planning, the AI copilot offers pre-meeting analysis and real-time insights during planning meetings.

The Outcome

TechFin Solutions saw notable changes three months of integration:

30% Reduction in Sprint Planning Time: Pre-meeting preparation by the AI copilot eliminated much of the information collecting and early prioritizing effort previously consuming meeting time, therefore reducing the sprint planning time.

Improved Team Clarity: Thanks to improved data-driven decision making, team members said they better understood sprint goals and their individual contributions.

Higher Sprint Success Rate: Improved capacity planning and risk identification helped to drive the rise in sprint performance from 68% to 84%, mostly toward attaining stated goals.

Enhanced Predictability: More precise forecasting based on past trends and present team state helped stakeholders to have trust in delivery times.

Important Success Components

Many elements helped to ensure the successful integration:

Gradual Adoption: The team first added artificial intelligence capabilities gradually instead of doing a total overhaul all at once.

Human Oversight: Team members checked and evaluated all AI recommendations so preserving human agency in decision-making.

Continuous Feedback: The team gave constant comments to guarantee the AI's recommendations stayed current and to help them to progress.

Change Management: Leaders spent time outlining the AI's role and addressing team worries about automation substituting for human judgment.

What AI Should Not Do: Setting Appropriate Boundaries

Although artificial intelligence copilots have many advantages, Agile teams must be aware of their constraints and set reasonable limits for their application.

Decision-Making Autonomy

Not replace human decision-making, AI copilots should improve it. Important decisions on strategic priorities, team makeup, and product development call for human judgment based on ethical considerations, corporate values, and long-term vision that artificial intelligence systems cannot completely understand; that which transcends data trends.

Why This Matters: Agile stresses human judgment and adaptation, therefore this matters. Let AI make autonomous judgments would compromise Agile's collaborative and flexible character.

Practical Implementation: Establish explicit procedures whereby artificial intelligence offers recommendations and analysis while humans make ultimate decisions and can reject AI advice where suitable.

Human Originality and Innovation

Artificial intelligence copilots struggle with real creativity and innovation while excelling in pattern identification and optimization. They should not be expected to replace human creativity, creative problem-solving, or brainstorming that generates original ideas driving forward solutions.

Why This Matters: Current artificial intelligence systems cannot reproduce the unexpected connections and creative leaps from which innovation often results. Dependency too much on AI recommendations could result in small changes while lost revolutionary prospects.

Practical Implementation: Use artificial intelligence to perform regular analysis and preparation so free (to free up) human team members to concentrate on creative and strategic tasks where they provide special value.

Contextual Thinking and Critical Thought

AI may overlook crucial contextual elements or complex scenarios requiring human knowledge even if it can rapidly handle enormous volumes of data. Edge case, ethical conundrums, and business context critical thinking should still mostly fall to human obligations.

Why This Matters: Agile teams work in challenging settings where optimal solutions depend on context and subtlety. AI systems might not know the whole ramifications of their suggestions.

Practical Implementation: Particularly in new or high-stakes scenarios, teach team members to challenge and verify AI advice.

Best Approaches for Leveraging AI Copilots

Effective integration of artificial intelligence copilots into Agile teams calls for careful preparation and continuous attention to technical as well as human aspects.

Start Small: Gradual Expanding Pilot Projects

- Start with low-risk applications, such meeting summaries or basic code recommendations, using AI copilots for activities with defined success criteria and limited possible negative impact.
- Start with team members who are eager about artificial intelligence integration and who can offer helpful criticism during the first phase of deployment.
- Clearly define success criteria and routinely evaluate if integration of artificial intelligence is producing anticipated results.

- Expand AI copilot use to other jobs and team members depending on proven value in first applications.

Train Teams: Developing AI Literacy

- Make sure every team member knows what artificial intelligence copilots can and cannot accomplish, therefore avoiding both over-reliance and underutilization.
- Teach team members how to work effectively with AI copilators, including how to evaluate recommendations and offer helpful comments, thereby promoting productive collaboration.
- Acknowledge team members' worries about artificial intelligence substituting for human roles and explicitly explain how AI will improve rather than replace human capacity.
- Provide team members chances to remain current on AI capabilities and best practices as the technology develops.

Embed Ethics: Responsible AI Integration

- Track for bias in AI recommendations and set procedures to find and fix troubling trends.
- Choose AI copilots that can clarify their recommendations and set procedures for team members to grasp the rationale behind AI recommendations.

- Maintaining accountability means precisely assigning responsibility for decisions taken with AI support and guaranteeing human supervision of AI-driven operations.
- Implement suitable data security policies and make sure AI copilots handle private data in line.

Transforming Agile Ceremonies with AI

- Though keep human facilitation and engagement, use AI to prepare meeting summaries and pinpoint discussion themes.
- While ensuring human debate and decision-making drives real changes, use artificial intelligence to examine team communication trends and recommend improvement areas.
- Use AI for capacity predictions and story prioritizing advice but keep cooperative planning conversations and human ultimate decisions even as you optimize sprint planning.
- Using artificial intelligence to examine user comments and usage statistics will help augment sprint reviews; yet human interpretation and stakeholder communication remain absolutely vital for the review process.

AI-Augmented Agile Teams: Future Development

Future integration of artificial intelligence copilots into Agile teams will probably grow and get more complex. One should anticipate:

- Development of AI systems especially meant for individual Agile jobs with great awareness of role-specific difficulties and processes results in more specialized artificial intelligence copilots.
- AI systems that can coordinate and distribute insights among several teams will help to improve organizational alignment and knowledge sharing by so facilitating cross-team intelligence.
- Advanced analytics able to forecast team performance problems and propose solutions before they completely materialize can help with predictive team health.
- Artificial intelligence copilots that constantly enhance their recommendations depending on team-specific results and preferences.

Important Lessons

Remember these key ideas as we wrap out our investigation of AI copilots in Agile teams:

- AI copilots improve Agile methods without substituting artificial intelligence for the human components that enable Agile success. While maintaining Agile's collaborative, flexible, and human-centred qualities, they offer data, insights, and automation.
- Although personalized AI support helps every Agile function, the particular applications and advantages depend greatly on the team context and role responsibility.

- Success calls more on augmentation than on automation. Rather than replace human judgment and creativity, the most successful implementations use artificial intelligence to magnify human strengths.
- Integration should be slow and deliberate, with regard to change management, education, and ongoing AI system enhancement grounded on team comments and results.
- Including artificial intelligence copilots on your Agile DNA team calls for constant learning, adaption, and ethical application methods

In the next chapter, we will examine how artificial intelligence is changing particular Agile ceremonies, making stand-ups more perceptive, sprint planning more accurate, and retrospectives more data-driven while preserving the collaborative spirit that makes these rituals effective.

CHAPTER 4: SUPER-CHARMONIES:

SUPERCHARGING SPRIINTS, BETTER STAND-UPS

Smaters Tand on The Vœahers

4

SUPERCHARGING CEREMONIES

SMARTER SPRINTS, BETTER STAND-UPS

INTRODUCTION: FROM RITUAL TO INTELLIGENCE

Imagine a normal Monday morning stand-up in which team members join a video chat or shuffle into a conference room and each individual recites what they did yesterday, what they intend to do today, and notes any obstacles. The Scrum Master faithfully notes, perhaps fixes a few tickets, and everyone goes back to work. By Tuesday, half of the conversation is lost, trends go unappreciated, and the same obstacles return week after week.

Imagine now a different situation: an artificial intelligence assistant has already examined the weekend's code updates, found developing trends in the backlog, and warned three possible bottlenecks using dependency analysis as the team assembles. The discussion centers on fixing problems, streamlining processes, and making strategic decisions guided by data unseen to human view rather than status updates.

This change marks Agile ceremonies' development from regular check-ins to intelligence-driven teamwork events. Daily stand-ups, sprint planning, reviews, and retrospectives encourage transparency, alignment, and ongoing improvement; agile ceremonies have always been the pulse of team communication and delivery rhythm. But in the fast-paced, data-rich environments of today, manual rituals are insufficient to reflect the complexity and speed of contemporary development activity.

Artificial intelligence accentuates rather than replaces these human-centred rituals. AI changes ceremonies from time-consuming responsibilities into insight-driven, time-efficient, and value-focused experiences teams really look forward to attending by bringing automation, prediction, and pattern recognition to the center of every Agile event.

How AI Improves Agile Ceremonies: The Intelligence Layer

Including artificial intelligence into Agile ceremonies results in what we might refer to as a "intelligence layer"; a data-driven basis guiding human conversation and decision-making. Operating constantly in the background, this layer analyzes data from several sources and surfaces insights exactly at the proper times in team operations.

The Data Sources Driving Ceremonies Enhanced by AI

Every day activities of modern Agile teams produce massive volumes of data:

Development Activity: Code commits, pull requests, code reviews, build results, and deployment metrics

Project Management: Story progress, time tracking, sprint velocity, and backlog changes

Communication: Slack messages, email threads, meeting transcripts, and documentation updates

User Feedback: Customer support tickets, product analytics, user surveys, and app store reviews

Team Dynamics: Meeting participation, communication sentiment, and collaboration patterns

Continuous processing of this data by artificial intelligence systems allows them to spot trends and patterns that would be impossible for people to manually monitor over several projects and timescale.

The Capabilities for Intelligence

Agile ceremonies gain some important powers from artificial intelligence:

- Over several sprints and teams, pattern recognition helps one identify recurrent themes, bottlenecks, and success elements.
- Forecasting likely results depending on past data and present patterns in predictive analytics.

- Understanding and producing human language for summaries, insights, and suggestions calls for natural language processing.
- Sentiment analysis helps one find emotional undertones in team conversations and comments.
- Combining data from several sources into logical, practical ideas is known as automated synthesis.

1. Daily Stand-ups: From Talk to Insights

Though it's usually the most mundane and least interesting Agile ritual, the daily stand-up is maybe thc most regular one. AI can make these quick encounters from status reporting events strategic problem-solving dialogues.

Conventional Stand-up Challenges

Typical stand-ups have various flaws:

Information Overload: Team members battle to recall and communicate all they have done. **Shallow Notes:** Emphasize actions instead of results or obstacles.

Pattern Blindness: Gradually over time, recurrent problems go unreported.

Time Inefficiency: Notable meeting time invested on data that could be obtained automatically

AI-Driven Improve Stand-up Enhancement

AI solves these problems by highlighting what really counts and automating data collecting:

Intelligent Advancement Summaries

AI may automatically create tailored progress summaries by analysing rather than asking "What did you do yesterday?"

- Git codes and commits.
- Jira ticket changes in status and updates.
- Code reviews and pull requests activity
- Slack messages and communication threads

Real-World Implementation: Spotify makes use of an artificial intelligence system to create pre-meeting summaries for every team member, therefore stressing their important contributions, teamwork styles, and possible issues. This lets stand-ups concentrate more on strategic conversations than on status reports.

Active Blocker Identification

Through analysis, artificial intelligence can spot possible obstacles before they become significant barriers:

- Measuring codes' complexity and review cycle
- Dependencies between epics and tales
- Team member availability trends and workload
- External dependence and failure rates

A machine learning system tracks Azure DevOps activity and automatically flags when a story has been "In Progress" for longer than usual completion times, when several team members are working on linked tasks that might conflict, or when outside dependencies show indications of instability.

Team Surveillance of Health

Beyond mere technical advancement, artificial intelligence can monitor team dynamics and welfare:

Communication Sentiment: Examining team communication tone helps one to spot stress, annoyance, or disengagement.

Participation Patterns: Tracking who participates in conversations and who stays quiet helps one see patterns of behaviour.

Workload Balance: Finding team members possibly overused or underused

Collaboration Quality: Measuring the frequency and potency of cross-team encounters helps to determine collaboration quality.

Voice-to-Text and Analysis Integration

Real-time stand-up discussion transcription in modern artificial intelligence systems allows for actionable information extraction:

- Record actions and commitments automatically.
- Determine whether outside the stand-up further conversations are required.
- Track whether previously indicated obstacles are clearing themselves.
- Create team reference searchable summaries.

Implementation Example: Using Otter.ai linked with their project management system, a software consulting transcribes stand-ups, automatically generates follow-up activities, and tracks the removal of issues raised in past meetings. While improving action item completion rates by 60%, this integration shortened their average stand-up time from 15 minutes to 8 minutes.

2. Sprint Planning: Smarter Scoping and Forecasting

Usually depending mostly on human judgment, historical trends, and best-guess predictions, sprint planning While maintaining the cooperative character of planning sessions, artificial intelligence lends data-driven accuracy to these important judgments.

The Development of Sprint Planning Wisdom

Study of Historical Patterns

Years of sprint data can be analysed by artificial intelligence algorithms to find trends guiding more informed planning decisions:

- **Story Completion Patterns**: Which kinds of stories regularly span more than expected?
- **Team Velocity Trends:** Composition, outside influences, and story mix all affect team effectiveness.
- **Spillover Predictors**: Story traits that often translate to later sprints: spillover predictors
- **Success Correlations**: Characteristics most likely to be successful when combined

Intelligent Prioritizing for Stories

AI can include several data sources for prioritizing recommendations instead of depending just on the input of business stakeholders:

- Processing user comments, support tickets, and use data helps one to find features addressing actual consumer pain issues.
- Examining code complexity, dependability relationships, and historical defect rates helps one to find tales with more implementation hazards.
- Linking feature delivery to business indicators

helps one to identify the kinds of activities that generate most organizational value.
- Ensuring story choice fits longer-term product strategy and organizational objectives guarantees strategic alignment.

Planning with Predictive Capability

Artificial intelligence can more precisely project team capacity than conventional velocity averaging:

- Examining each team member's talents, present workload, scheduled time off, and past performance patterns helps one to build individual capacity.
- Factoring in the possibility of delays from outside teams, outside vendors, or infrastructure improvements influences external dependency.
- Using machine learning models educated on past narrative completion data, complexity-adjusted estimates can be more accurate effort estimates.
- Including uncertainty ranges instead of point estimations will help to increase the dependability of the planning.

Real-world sprint planning improvement:

Case Study: AI-Enhanced Planning System at TechCorp

Using AI-enhanced sprint planning, a mid-sized technological company produced amazing results:

Prior to AI Integration:

- Two-week sprints averaged four hours for sprint planning sessions.
- Of the sprints, 35% underwent notable scope adjustments midway through.
- 68% of the time sprint goals were met.
- Teams either over- or under-commit to their job regularly.

After AI Integration:

- Sprint planning time down to 2.5 hours yields improved results.
- Over sprints, scope dropped to 18%.
- Achieving a sprint objective raised to 84%
- Accuracy in work commitment greatly improved

Important artificial intelligence skills applied:

- AI produced recommendations including story prioritizing, capacity estimates, and risk assessments 24 hours before planning meetings.
- AI gave real-time comments on suggested narrative combinations, highlighting potential conflicts or overcommitting, during planning meetings.
- The system used results from every sprint to enhance future recommendations, therefore forming a feedback loop that over time produced more accurate forecasts.

3. Sprint Reviews: Intelligent Feedback and Demo Analytics

Two uses for sprint reviews include celebrating finished work and compiling comments from stakeholders for next versions. AI can improve both by offering better understanding of past achievements and future directions.

Beyond Conventions in Demos

Many times, traditional sprint reviews suffer from:

- Surface comments devoid of driving significant product enhancements
- Challenge linking feature delivery to corporate results.
- Limited view of user acceptance and satisfaction
- Oversaw missed chances to pinpoint strategic pivots or improvements

Review Capabilities Enhanced by Artificial Intelligence

Automated Demo Notes

From sprint reviews, artificial intelligence can gather and arrange data:

- Finding significant events and stakeholder responses during demos highlights extraction.
- Automatically gathering stakeholder questions and concerns for follow-up in a catalogue of questions and ıssues

- Connecting shown features to user stories and corporate goals helps to create feature impact summaries.
- Analysing comments tone and degree of enthusiasm helps one understand stakeholder sentiment.

Integration for Real-Time Usage Analytics

Living usage data can be included into sprint reviews by modern artificial intelligence systems:

- Showing how recently implemented features are being used by actual production customers helps to track feature adoption.
- Using measurements like conversion rates, user engagement, or operational efficiency, performance effect analysis shows the commercial value of certain features.
- Integrating user feedback for pertinent client comments, support tickets, or app store ratings pertaining to shown capabilities.
- Contextualizing the delivery of features against competitor offerings in the market will help to clarify their difference.

Clever Follow-Up Suggestions

AI can recommend next sprint priorities depending on usage statistics and demo comments:

- Stories addressing issues mentioned throughout the review
- Improvements that might magnify the effect of effective traits
- Pivots grounded on surprising user behaviour or feedback patterns
- Technical debt elements with potential enhancement of feature performance

Implementation Example: E-commerce Platform Reviews

An e-commerce platform team included artificial intelligence into their sprint assessments and produced really remarkable outcomes:

Demo Analytics Powered by AI:

- Real-time showing of feature usage statistics during demos
- Automatic correlation between changes in conversion rate and given features
- Combining consumer comments on newly introduced features
- Predictive study of feature influence on important corporate indicators

Outcomes:

- 40% increase in participation of stakeholders during evaluations

- 25% rise in the business value of later sprint activity
- Three weeks on average less time from feedback to implementation
- More harmony between corporate goals and development projects

4. Retrospectives: Data-Powered Reflection

Though they sometimes suffer from recency bias, group-think, and weak analysis, retrospectives are perhaps the most crucial Agile ceremony for ongoing improvement. Retrospection can be turned by artificial intelligence into data-driven improvement sessions pushing significant change.

Conventional Retrospection Restrictions

Typical retro difficulties include:

- Emphasize recent occurrences while neglecting more long-term trends.
- Dominant voices overwhelm quieter team members in participation.
- Talking about symptoms instead than underlying causes
- Developing swiftly forgotten improvement ideas

AI-Enhanced Retrospective Capabilities

Comprehensive Sprint Analysis

Unlike depending on human memory, artificial intelligence can examine the whole sprint period:

- Examining team chat logs, email threads, and meeting transcripts helps one to spot communication efficacy, problem areas, and patterns of cooperation or lack.
- Tracking how tales passed through several states helps one to find process inefficiencies and bottlenecks.
- Examining the emotional tone of team discussions across the sprint helps one to spot stress areas and patterns in satisfaction.
- Comparing present sprint patterns with historical data helps one to spot tendencies either improving or declining.

Anonymous Input Aggregation

By use of anonymous data collecting and analysis, artificial intelligence can enable more inclusive retrospectives:

- Before the meeting, pre-retroactive surveys asking anonymous comments on sprint problems, achievements, and improvement suggestions.
- Using natural language processing, theme clustering groups related feedback items and finds the most often mentioned problems.

- Examining the emotional tone of comments will help one rank the most important or interesting subjects.
- Tracking development on past retroactive projects and highlighting unsolved problems.

Real-World Retrospection and Transformation

Case Study: AI- Powered Retrospectives of Global Retail Company

Using artificial intelligence, a global retail corporation ran retrospectives across fifteen development teams:

Implementation Approach:

- Connected AI systems gathered thorough sprint data by linking Slack, Jira, GitHub, and meeting systems.
- Before meetings, use a conversational artificial intelligence bot to compile past comments using natural language dialogues.
- Designed visualizations displaying communication patterns, work flow efficiency, and sentiment trends throughout time on a Pattern Recognition Dashboard.
- Using artificial intelligence, track retroactive commitments and disclose unsolved problems in next sessions.

Results After Six Months:

- 45% increase in rates of retroactive action items completed.
- 30% less regular blocks across sprints
- Higher team satisfaction ratings, especially with regard to psychological safety measurements
- improved resolution of systematic problems influencing several teams and identification of them

Important Success Components:

- Teams began with simple AI summaries then added more advanced analysis tools.
- Transparency: Teams were given open access to all AI research with well-defined methods of generation of insights.
- AI gave facts and insights; human facilitators guided conversations and made decisions.
- Team comments and retroactive results helped the AI system itself to be constantly enhanced.

Beyond Automation: Promoting Improved Interaction

The real worth of artificial intelligence in Agile ceremonies is not only automation but also better human interactions and decision-making enabled by it. As an intelligent preparation and analysis layer, artificial intelligence lets teams concentrate on the most important discussions.

Exposing Hidden Patterns

Artificial intelligence can reveal insights difficult or impossible for humans to spot:

- Finding how changes in one team's output impact other teams or systems
- Examining long-term trends in team performance, contentment, or technical quality and noting slow changes in either
- Correlating team performance with outside elements like market conditions, organizational changes, or seasonal trends helps to identify impact.
- Identifying the characteristics of high-performing sprints and teams

Promoting Psychological Safety

AI can help to facilitate more inclusive team debates:

- Encouragement of team members to express ideas or problems without regard to criticism or reprisal results in anonymous contribution.
- Finding when some team members are not participating in conversations and providing chances for their opinions is part of balanced participation.
- Offering data-driven insights emphasizing systemic problems and thereby lessening the personal character of comments.

- Rather than viewing present difficulties as isolated failures, help teams grasp them in the framework of their path of improvement.

Fostering Accountability with Follow-Up Tracking

AI systems can preserve institutional memory allowing teams to keep their promises:

- Monitoring progress on ceremonial enhancements and retroactive obligations forms an action item.
- Noting when teams revert to past behaviours and proposing remedies
- Highlighting when modifications produce better results will help to motivate further development.
- Alerting when team-level problems need for organizational support or attention

Tools in Action: The Ceremony Toolkit Enhanced by AI

Many technologies have surfaced to assist Agile ceremonies augmented by artificial intelligence, each with unique features and integration possibilities:

Integrated Platform Solutions

- Across Atlassian tools, Jira Intelligence offers AI-powered summaries, recommendations for backlog prioritizing, and pattern identification. Especially robust for companies already engaged in the Atlassian ecosystem.

- Offering predictive capacity planning, intelligent work item recommendations, and automated reporting capabilities linked with Microsoft's development platform, Azure DevOps AI.
- Monday.com AI: For teams running their project management tool, delivers predictive timeline changes, automated status updates, and smart project insights.

Tool for Specialized Ceremonies

- Designed especially for daily stand-ups, ScrumGenius is an AI-powered stand-up helper with mood tracking, automated summaries, and pattern identification.
- Combining sentiment tracking, anonymous input aggregation, dialog analysis, and retrospective facilitation, TeamRetro + AI Plugins
- Otter.ai + Integration Tools: Available with many project management and collaboration systems, offers real-time transcribing and analysis.

Platforms for Communication and Analysis

- Miro AI improves collaborative whiteboarding with intelligent content production, template recommendations, and meeting facilitation tools.
- Custom AI integrations that examine team communication habits and offer information for ceremonial planning; slack analytics plus custom bots

- Microsoft Viva Insights offers team collaboration analytics and ideas for enhancing team well-being and meeting efficacy.

Guidelines for AI-Enhanced Ceremonies

Effective integration of artificial intelligence into Agile ceremonies calls both technical implementation and change management great attention.

Technical Implementation Strategies

- Start with Integration, not Replacement: Rather than entirely rebuilding current ceremonies, start by applying AI to improve upon them. This lowers change resistance and lets teams progressively adopt new capabilities.
- AI insights are only as good as the data they are derived from. Spend time making sure your staff keeps strong data hygiene standards and that your tools are set up correctly.
- Teams should be transparent about how artificial intelligence recommendations are produced and be able to challenge or reject them as needed.
- Maintaining human agency, artificial intelligence should not replace but rather inform and assist human decision-making. Make sure team members keep influence over team procedures and ceremony results.

Considerations in Change Management

- Early-stage Agile teams might gain more from simple process development before adding AI sophistication. Usually, more advanced teams can manage complicated artificial intelligence integration more successfully.
- Transparency regarding the data AI systems gather and evaluate will help to address privacy issues. Make sure team members find the degree of analysis and monitoring being used appealing.
- Help team members interpret AI-generated insights and operate successfully with ceremonies improved by artificial intelligence.
- Regularly evaluate if AI improvements are adding value, then modify deployment depending on team comments and evolving needs.

Strategies for Cultural Integration:

- Present artificial intelligence as a co-facilitator; a team member who offers specialized analysis instead of a management tool or substitute for human judgment.
- Show every team member AI analysis instead of only Scrum Masters or team leads. This fosters confidence and clarifies team patterns for all.
- While artificial intelligence offers insightful data, make sure to still address team relationships, motivation, and job satisfaction even if it depends on emotional intelligence.

- AI integration could be more welcome to some team members than others. Let people accept gradually and respect their different comfort levels.

Important Notes

As we wrap up our investigation of Agile ceremonies augmented by artificial intelligence, some important realizations surface:

- Because they produce rich data streams and benefit from pattern recognition that humans struggle to execute manually, agile rituals are perfect candidates for AI augmentation.
- By uncovering hidden patterns, forecasting anticipated outcomes, and supporting data-informed decisions, artificial intelligence changes ceremonies from mundane check-ins to insight-driven collaboration sessions.
- Rather than substituting, the most effective implementations center on improving human interaction. AI offers the intelligence basis that lets teams have more meaningful interactions.
- Rather of forcing teams to adopt whole new platforms or procedures, tool choice should give top priority to smooth interface with current systems.
- Introducing AI-enhanced ceremonies calls for change management just as much as technological execution. Teams require help,

instruction, and slow introduction to new skills.

- Though artificial intelligence supports and guides team engagement, it cannot replace the cooperative connections that make Agile ceremonies successful. The human touch is still absolutely vital.

Through technologies like India's BharatGen project and other multilingual AI systems, we will investigate in the following chapter how artificial intelligence is tearing down linguistic and cultural boundaries in Agile teams, therefore enabling more inclusive and productive cooperation across worldwide companies.

Chapter 5:
Going Global
Making Agile Work In Any Language

5

GOING GLOBAL

MAKING AGILE WORK IN ANY LANGUAGE

INTRODUCTION: THE UNIVERSAL LANGUAGE OF AGILITY

Imagine this: A global software development company works out Bangalore, São Paulo, and Munich. Priya feels most at ease describing a difficult technical barrier in Hindi during their daily stand-up; Carlos wants to express his creative idea in Portuguese, and Hans has vital insights he would best be able to communicate in German. In conventional Agile configurations, these important contributions could be lost in translation; that is, literally; or team members might just remain quiet instead of working on English as a second language.

Agile is about people, teamwork, and common understanding mostly. It's a way of thinking anchored in ideals and ideas that cut across language and cultural barriers. The Agile Manifesto emphasizes universal values; that of "individuals and interactions over processes and tools" and "customer collaboration over contract negotiation"; that transcend language.

Still, the pragmatic reality of most Agile implementations stays relentlessly English-centric in spite of these universal ideas. From Jira templates to Scrum manuals, from retrospective approaches to user story templates, the tools and frameworks teams use daily default English. Subtle but important barriers resulting from this linguistic prejudice might exclude important voices, lower engagement, and finally compromise team performance.

This terrain is being profoundly altered by the emergence of inclusive AI technologies, especially multilingual natural language processing systems such as India's BharatGen project. These sophisticated artificial intelligence algorithms grasp domain-specific language across dozens of languages, context, and cultural nuances in addition to translating words. In ways that were unthinkable only a few years ago, they are making Agile really accessible, collaborative, and locally tailored.

This chapter looks at how more inclusive participation, language hurdles in Agile teams being broken down by AI-powered multilingual capabilities, and companies releasing the full potential of their worldwide workforce are being facilitated.

Language Obstacles: The Agile Challenge

Agile teams are spread over several nations, cultures, and languages more and more since modern software development is worldwide. Although this variety offers great advantages in terms of viewpoint, knowledge, and market awareness, it also presents major obstacles that can compromise Agile's basic values.

The extent of the difficulty

Geographic Distribution: GitLab's 2024 Remote Work Report shows that 42% of software development teams span four or more time zones and linguistic areas while 73% of teams now include members from at least three different locations.

Language Diversity in Tech Hubs: Major technology hubs including Bangalore, Tel Aviv, Berlin, and Singapore are naturally multilingual settings where team members may be fluent in several languages but still prefer their home tongue for difficult technical conversations.

Cultural Communication Styles: Beyond language, different cultures have distinct ways to address hierarchy, directness, and conflict resolution that could influence Agile ceremonial participation and efficacy.

Specific Barriers in Agile Contexts

Reduced Participation in Ceremonies

Many negative consequences follow from team members having to communicate in a non-native tongue:

Cognitive Load: Speaking in one language while thinking in another calls for more mental work, therefore reducing cognitive capacity for the real substance of conversations.

Simplified Expression: When team members lack confidence in their English expression skills, complicated concepts could be excluded totally or oversimplified.

Time Delays: Formulating ideas in a second language takes more time, hence fast-paced rituals like stand-ups could seem hurried or insufficient.

Cultural Hesitation: Many societies view group speaking as requiring more confidence, hence language difficulties exacerbate this hesitation.

Documentation and Knowledge Transfer Difficulties

•**Template Limitations**: Standard Agile templates for user stories, acceptance criteria, and retrospective formats are created around English phrase structures and may not translate effectively conceptually to other languages.

•**information Silos:** When team members cannot successfully convey specialized ideas across language barriers, critical domain information may remain caught inside language groups.

•**Decision Context Loss**: When team members fail to express difficult explanations in English, the rationale behind significant decisions may be inadequately recorded.

Engagement of Stakeholders Problems

- **Customer Voice Dilution**: Nuances and emotional context are sometimes lost when customer comments have to be passed through several layers.
- **Local Market Insights**: Deep knowledge of local markets among team members might not enable them to adequately share these findings with worldwide product teams.
- **Requirement Misunderstanding**: Little variations in how requirements are understood across languages could result in development effort lacking the necessary quality.

Language Obstacles: Their Cost

Studies published in the Harvard Business Review show that teams with notable language hurdles suffer:

- 23% longer sprint planning sessions yielding less successful results
- Thirty-one percent less completion of retrospective action items
- 18% more rework brought on by misinterpreted needs
- Reduced team performance ratings, especially for non-native English speakers

These effects reflect missed innovation, lower engagement, and unrealized potential inside development teams; not only operational ones.

Enter BharatGen: India's Open-Source Multilingual AI

With India's BharatGen project, artificial intelligence is being really multilingual and culturally conscious; a first. BharatGen is made to grasp the cultural context, subject expertise, and collaborative nuances necessary for successful Agile cooperation, not unlike translating technologies that just translate words from one language to another.

The Methodology of BharatGen: Technology

- BharatGen has been taught on around 22 Indian languages, including Hindi, Bengali, Telugu, Marathi, Tamil, Gujarati, Kannada, Malayalam, Odia, Punjabi, and many more. This article captures the language reality of the technological workforce in India.
- Beyond simple translating, BharatGen is aware of cultural communication patterns, hierarchical relationships, and indirect communication techniques typical of Indian commercial environments.
- The system has been especially trained on business terms, Agile methodology, and software development to guarantee that technical ideas are faithfully expressed across languages.

- BharatGen can process text and speech in real-time, therefore facilitating smooth multilingual dialogues free from the delays linked with conventional translating systems.
- Crucially for good team communication, the AI keeps context throughout dialogues, understands allusions, pronouns, and implicit meaning.

Agile-Specific Capabilities: BharatGen

- Agile ceremonies in several languages can be facilitated by the system, which lets team members engage in their choice language while guaranteeing everyone understands the main ideas.
- Technical accuracy and business intent are preserved even while user stories, acceptance criteria, and other Agile artifacts are automatically translated.
- BharatGen can identify emotional undertones and team dynamics across many languages, so offering facilitators understanding of team health independent of the language being utilized.
- Agile techniques are adapted by the system to fit local cultural settings while keeping the fundamental ideas and success of the approaches.

How Multilingual AI Enhances Agile

Multilingual artificial intelligence integration into Agile processes offers chances for more inclusive, efficient, and culturally sensitive team cooperation. Let's look at this across several Agile ceremonies and activities.

•Daily Stand-ups: Breaking Down Communication Barriers

When team members struggle to communicate difficult technical ideas in English, traditional stand-ups can suffer. Multilingual artificial intelligence turns these gatherings into really inclusive debates.

Translating Real-Time Synthesizing

- Team members can converse in their native tongue while others get real-time translations in their preferred language under seamless language switching. Over these language exchanges, the AI keeps context.
- Agile-specific AI preserves the meaning of technical terminology, methodological principles, and domain-specific language unlike most general translation tools.
- The AI can create meeting summaries in several languages, therefore guaranteeing that every team member has access to important data independent of the languages used during the conversation.

Cultural Communication Enhancement

- Many societies value indirect communication techniques that could be misinterpreted in English-only settings. AI can properly interpret and transmit these nuanced messages.

- Maintaining Agile's collaborative values, the system recognizes cultural hierarchies and can help to provide comfortable communication patterns for all team members.

2. Retrospectives: Enabling Authentic Reflection

Retrospectives demand honest, careful analysis of team performance and issues. Language limitations can impede team members from sharing sensitive issues or nuanced insights.

Anonymous Multilingual Input

- Through text or speech, team members can offer retroactive comments in their original tongue, therefore guaranteeing that difficult concepts are thoroughly expressed.
- Understanding team dynamics and tackling fundamental problems depend on the emotional context of input, which the artificial intelligence preserves.
- The technology can find shared issues and themes even in several languages, therefore giving team health facilitators complete understanding.

Retroactive Formats: Cultural Adaptation

- Retrospective templates and models can be customized to fit cultural communication preferences while still being successful for ongoing development.

- The AI can help negotiate cultural variations in how conflicts are presented and handled so that all points of view are heard and acknowledged.

3. Sprint Demos and Reviews: Inclusive Stakeholder Engagement

Review of sprints sometimes include people from many areas and cultural backgrounds. Multilingual artificial intelligence guarantees that feedback is precisely recorded and interpreted as well as that all voices are heard.

Integration of Stakeholder Comments

•Stakeholders can submit comments in their native tongue, therefore guaranteeing that cultural subtleties and market-specific insights are faithfully recorded.

- By synthesizing comments from many languages and civilizations, the AI may find common themes while maintaining original regional points of view.
- Post-review communications can be carried out in the chosen languages of stakeholders, therefore ensuring that development teams clearly grasp the needs.

4. Documentation: Multilingual Knowledge Management

Agile teams produce plenty of documentation that must be available to every team member regardless of language preferences.

Translating Living Documentation

- Technical documentation, acceptance criteria, and user stories may all be automatically translated and maintained current as changes come around.
- Technical ideas and commercial sense are kept across translations to guarantee that the aim and content stay whole.
- Team members can search for information in their preferred language and locate pertinent material independent of the language in which it was first produced.

Real-World Impact: Case Studies in Multilingual Agile

Case Study 1: Public Sector Digital Transformation in India

BharatGen-powered Agile methods were applied by a sizable public sector company in India across twelve development teams working on citizen service projects.

The Challenge: Teams comprised developers fluent in Hindi, Tamil, Bengali, English, and other regional languages whereas stakeholders would rather interact in several regional languages. Conventional English-only Agile methods were lowering citizen-focused solution quality and involvement.

The Application:

- Multilingual retrospectives allowing team members to voice issues in their native tongue
- Translating in real time during cross-team meetings
- Documentation accessible in many Indian languages
- Regional language stakeholder comments collecting with automatic synthesis

The Results:

- 60% increase in rates of retrospectives participation
- 45% increase in citizen stakeholders' actionable comments
- 32% less cycles of requirement clarification
- Greater team satisfaction levels among all language groups
- More culturally fitting answers for many different citizen groups

Case Study 2: Global E-commerce Platform Development

To enhance their Agile teamwork, a worldwide e-commerce firm with workers in Germany, Brazil, and India used multilingual artificial intelligence.

The challenge: English-speaking team members dominated product choices, but language hurdles were underutilizing important local market expertise.

The Application:

- Multilingual product planning meetings with instantaneous translation
- Cultural adaptation of user story forms to local communication media
- Cross-cultural reflections using sentiment analysis across several languages
- Integrating customer comments in many languages into sprint reviews

The Results:

- 40% boost in non-English markets' feature adoption rates
- better fit of products for several cultural settings
- 28% less events of cultural misunderstandings
- Better employee involvement ratings among non-native English speakers

Other Tools Supporting Multilingual Agile

Although BharatGen marks a major innovation in multilingual artificial intelligence for Agile teams, several other technologies and platforms are driving this change as well:

Integration Solutions for Enterprises

- Real-time translation features of Google Cloud Translation AI with Workspace Integration combine with Google Workspace technologies usually used by Agile teams; Docs, Sheets, and Meet.
- Offering multilingual meeting transcription, translation, and sentiment analysis combined with Microsoft Teams and Azure DevOps, Microsoft Azure Cognitive Services for Teams
- Third-party plugins adding multilingual capability to Jira, Confluence, and other Atlassian apps mark the Marketplace Language Solutions.

Platforms of Specialized Communication

- **Vernacular.ai**: Especially helpful for distributed teams doing rituals over voice conversations, it centers on voice-based interactions in Indian languages.
- **AI4Bharat**: An open-source project called AI4Bharat offers speech-to-text capabilities for Indian languages, hence improving documentation and transcribing meeting capability.
- **DeepL API Integration**: With API integrations for several Agile products, known for excellent translations, especially for European languages.

New Cultural Adaptation Strategies

Systems that transcends translation to offer cultural communication direction and adaption advice represent cultural context artificial intelligence.

AI-powered technologies that recognize various cultural communication styles and may thus modify meeting facilitation are inclusive meeting facilitators.

Platforms that can gather and aggregate comments from several cultural settings while maintaining significant subtleties help to create cross-cultural feedback systems.

Guidelines for Using Multilingual Agile

Implementing multilingual artificial intelligence successfully in Agile teams needs both cultural sensitivity and meticulous preparation. Key behaviors like these help to ensure effective adoption:

Technical Execution

- **Start with High-Impact Ceremonies**: Start by using multilingual AI in retrospectives or stakeholder input sessions when language obstacles have the most effect.
- **Ensure Quality Translation**: Use artificial intelligence tools especially taught on Agile and software development terms instead of general-purpose translating technologies to guarantee quality.

- **Maintain Human Oversight**: Have bilingual team members confirm significant translations; especially for sensitive messages or key decisions.
- **Integrate with Existing Tools**: Choose solutions that fit your present Agile toolchain rather than calling for complete platform upgrades.

Cultural Considerations

- **Normalize Language Diversity:** Make it such that speaking native languages is valued rather than perceived as a hurdle to be surmounted.
- **Respect Communication Styles:** Know that Agile techniques should be modified depending on the ways in which different civilizations handle directness, hierarchy, and dispute resolution.
- **Provide Choice**: Let team members choose their preferred language for various kinds of contacts instead than requiring multilingual involvement.
- **Cultural Training**: Along with multilingual AI application, offer cross-cultural communication training to optimize impact.

Support Inside Organizations

- **Leadership Buy-in**: Make sure organizational leaders appreciate and support the value of multilingual Agile methods.
- **Resource Allocation**: Invest enough money in training, tool application, and continuous support of multilingual practices.

- **Measurement and Improvement**: Track participation rates, engagement scores, and other indicators to make sure multilingual artificial intelligence is really raising team effectiveness.
- **Community Building**: Create communities of practice centred on multilingual Agile implementation to distribute best practices and ideas.

Important Learnings

As we draw to an end our investigation of multilingual artificial intelligence in Agile methods, some crucial realizations show up:

- Agile team performance is strongly influenced by language hurdles, which lower participation, limit innovation, and cause unwarranted conflict in teams.
- Multilingual capabilities driven by artificial intelligence are revolutionizing worldwide Agile teams, allowing more inclusive involvement and improved use of many points of view and skill set.
- BharatGen and other new generation of culturally conscious artificial intelligence tools go beyond mere translation to offer real cross-cultural communication.
- Effective implementation calls for technical as well as cultural factors like respect of communication styles, organizational support, and slow adoption strategies.

- Beyond specific teams, the advantages cover organizational performance, better product-market fit, stakeholder involvement, and employee happiness among different worldwide workforce sizes.
- For companies able to fully utilize their worldwide staff, multilingual Agile is becoming a competitive advantage.

Our next chapter will look at how ethical, fair, and with suitable regard to privacy and cultural sensitivity responsible artificial intelligence processes guarantee the implementation of these great multilingual capabilities. Long-term success of AI-enhanced Agile methods depends on developing trust by means of responsible artificial intelligence application.

CHAPTER 6:

Building Trust with Responsible Responsible AI

Reobionion

6

BUILDING TRUST WITH RESPONSIBLE AI

INTRODUCTION: THE ETHICAL IMPERATIVE

A significant e-commerce firm found in 2023 that for more than two years their AI-powered recruiting tool had been methodically discriminating against women. Trained on historical employment data reflecting past prejudices, the algorithm learnt to downplay applications with terms like "women's" (as in "women's chess club captain") and give candidates from male-dominated universities top priority. Hundreds of qualified candidates had been wrongfully denied consideration by the time the bias was found, resulting in legal challenges, government investigation, and major reputational harm.

This example highlights a crucial reality: Agile teams have to deal with the significant ethical consequences of these potent technologies even as they embrace artificial intelligence to improve their processes, output, and decision making capacity. The same artificial intelligence technologies that can boost sprint planning, improve retrospectives, and maximize team performance can also support negative prejudices, violate privacy rights, and produce conclusions teams cannot defend or explain.

Many Agile transformations are motivated by speed and efficiency, which must be tempered with an equally strong dedication to safe artificial intelligence techniques. This goes beyond mere compliance or risk reduction to make sure the AI tools we include into our most basic team operations really support organizational ideals and human flourishing.

With their focus on openness, teamwork, and ongoing development, agile teams are especially suited to lead the way in ethical artificial intelligence application. While the collaborative culture of Agile teams helps the cross-functional communication required to find and resolve AI concerns, the iterative character of Agile workflows naturally provides ethical evaluation checkpoints.

This chapter looks at how Agile teams could establish trust by using responsible AI techniques, including ethical considerations into all facets of their AI-enhanced processes, so preserving the speed and efficiency that define Agile value.

Why Responsible AI Matters: The Stakes Are Higher Than Ever

Including artificial intelligence into Agile methods increases opportunities as well as risks. Motivating the investment in responsible procedures that good artificial intelligence governance calls for depends on an awareness of these stakes.

Fairness and Bias: The Amplification Problem

AI systems accentuate and systematize biases already present in training data, organizational processes, and human decision-making; they do not produce prejudice from nothing. This can show up in several Agile contexts:

- AI systems that suggest story priorities depending on past data could reinforce past prejudices about which customer segments or use cases get focus.
- AI systems that examine team communication patterns could unfairly punish team members whose communication styles deviate from historical standards, therefore discriminating against neurodiverse people or ethnic minorities.
- Artificial intelligence systems that synthesis consumer comments could give some demographic groups or communication styles undue weight, therefore biassing product judgments.

The difficulty is especially great as these prejudices frequently operate silently, buried in data patterns that seem objective yet represent past injustices.

Building Trust with Responsible AI

Transparency and Explainability: The Black Box Challenge

Particularly those built on deep learning, many artificial intelligence systems function as "black boxes" where the link between inputs and outputs is mathematically complicated and challenging to understand. In Agile settings, this opacity becomes troublesome when:

- Teams must clarify to stakeholders why particular suggestions were adopted or actions implemented.
- Teams must know why unexpected outcomes from AI-enhanced processes arise if they are to make improvements.
- Organizations must know how decisions affected by artificial intelligence were taken if those judgments backfire

- Agile teams excel on knowing what works and why, which calls for openness into artificial intelligence decision-making procedures.

Governance and Accountability: The Responsibility Vacuum

Questions of responsibility get more difficult as artificial intelligence systems grow more sophisticated and self-governing. Traditional Agile methods let teams follow choices back to particular people and interactions. AI presents a fresh class of "automated decisions" that might not clearly belong under human ownership.

This creates challenges for:

- Companies have to be able to show that they follow rules even if artificial intelligence technologies help with decisions.
- Teams must have processes in place to guarantee that artificial intelligence systems run under organizational values and ethical bounds.
- Teams must fast find reasons of problems and apply fixes when they arise.
- Agile teams must learn from AI system performance if they are to create next versions better.

Legal Compliance: Changing Legal Environment

The fast-changing regulatory environment around artificial

intelligence has major consequences for how Agile teams apply AI-enhanced technologies.

- The EU AI Act assigns risk categories; minimal, limited, high, and unacceptable risk, along with matching compliance criteria for AI systems. High-risk artificial intelligence systems call for human supervision, testing, and plenty of documentation.
- European data protection laws establish particular criteria for automated decision-making and profiling that influence artificial intelligence implementations.
- Industries such healthcare, banking, and transportation have particular needs for artificial intelligence systems that impact Agile teams in these areas' implementation.
- Countries all across are drafting artificial intelligence laws, which will complicate compliance for multinational companies.

What is Responsible AI? A Framework for Moral Application

Responsible artificial intelligence offers a complete method for designing, building, and implementing AI systems that give ethical issues top priority alongside technological excellence. This involves including ethical assessment and monitoring into every element of Agile teams' AI-enhanced processes.

Fundamental Ideas for Responsible AI

Non-Discrimination and Fairness

AI systems should treat every person and group fairly, therefore preventing both direct discrimination and unequal impact. In Agile environments, this implies:

- Making sure AI-enhanced procedures don't methodically disadvantage any team member or stakeholder group
- Routinely checking AI recommendations for bias across several demographic groups
- Building AI systems to encourage inclusive involvement instead than supporting current power relations

Privacy and Data Security

AI systems have to honour personal privacy rights and guard private data. Agile teams have to consider:

- What information artificial intelligence systems gather and how may it be applied?
- Whether team members have given their informed permission for AI study of their communications and work.
- How sensitive data is safeguarded along AI processing pipelines?
- Whether people have control over their information and AI-based observations of them

Openness and explainability

Stakeholders should be able to grasp how judgments made by artificial intelligence systems impact their own life. this covers:

- Clearly justifying AI advice and choices of action
- Clearly showing consumers AI system strengths and limits
- Recording methods, performance traits, and AI system training data
- Allowing participants to contest or appeal judgments motivated by artificial intelligence

Human Authority and Control

Especially for important judgments, humans should keep significant influence over artificial intelligence systems. Agile surroundings:

- AI should enhance rather than take over human judgment in important judgments.
- Teams should have systems to change or reject artificial intelligence advice.
- Well defined governance systems should specify when human review is needed.
- There should be escalation protocols for handling AI system issues.

Strongness and Security

AI systems should run safely and consistently in several environments and use scenarios:

- AI systems should smoothly handle unforeseen events.
- Performance should be constant among several user groups and situations.
- Systems should incorporate tracking and warning for odd activity.
- Frequent testing should confirm safety and performance of artificial intelligence systems.

Key Global Regulations Shaping Responsible AI

Agile teams using AI-enhanced technologies; especially those across international borders; must first understand the regulatory terrain.

European Union AI Act

Establishing a risk-based approach to AI governance, the EU AI Act is the first thorough AI law in history:

System for Classifying Risk:

- Unacceptable Risk: AI systems banned for threatening rights, livelihoods, or safety
- High Risk: AI systems applied in employment, transportation, or healthcare (strict criteria) or in other important sectors.

- Limited Risk: AI systems interacting with humans (requiring openness)
- Minimal Risk: Every other artificial intelligence system; self-regulation promoted;

High-Risk Systems: Compliance Guidelines

- Risk evaluation and mitigating strategies
- premium training sets with bias detection
- Comprehensive records and documentation
- open material for consumers
- Demand for human supervision
- Testing accuracy and strength

OECD AI Norms

AI principles developed by the Organization for Economic Cooperation and Development center on:

- AI should improve human capacities and creativity, therefore benefiting the earth and mankind.
- Throughout the AI system life, artificial intelligence agents should honour democratic values, human rights, and the law.
- AI actors should pledge openness and responsible disclosure about AI systems.
- AI systems should operate suitably and not create unjustified safety concerns.
- AI actors should answer for the appropriate operation of their systems.

Ethical AI Policies in India

The way India approaches artificial intelligence ethics stresses:

- AI systems ought to be made to be inclusive and easily available to every part of society.
- AI should not support or magnify society prejudices or discrimination.
- Transparency: AI systems should run their operations and make decisions with openness.
- Clear systems of responsibility should apply for the results of artificial intelligence systems.
- Individual privacy rights should be safeguarded in applications of artificial intelligence.

Embedding Responsible AI into Agile Workflows

Agile's iterative, cooperative approach offers natural chances to incorporate appropriate artificial intelligence techniques. Teams can include responsible AI issues into current Agile rituals and artifacts instead of seeing ethics as an isolated issue.

Backlog Grooming: Ethical Personal Narratives

While conventional user stories mostly address functional needs, responsible artificial intelligence calls for deliberate attention to ethical issues:

Transparency Stories: "As a user, I want to understand how the AI system made its recommendation so that I might make informed decisions."

Fairness Stories: As a product manager, I want to make sure that AI recommendations don't methodically disadvantage any user category so that we retain fair service.

Privacy Stories: "As a team member, I want control over what personal data is used for AI analysis so that my privacy is protected," says one privacy story.

Oversight Stories: As a team lead, I want to be able to evaluate and override AI judgments so that human judgment remains key to significant choices.

Sprint Planning: Giving Ethical Attributes Top Priority

Sessions of sprint planning should specifically include responsible artificial intelligence aspects in addition to functional development:

- Allocating time for methodical testing of AI outputs across several demographic groups and application cases helps to expose bias.
- Prioritizing elements that make artificial intelligence decision-making more transparent and understandable can help to explainability development.
- Tracking AI performance and spotting possible ethical concerns in manufacturing will help to build systems.
- Creating appropriate artificial intelligence documentation including data nutrition labels, model cards, and other tools.

Sprint Reviews: Ethical Stakeholder Evaluation

Sprint reviews give stakeholders chances to participate on ethical aspects of artificial intelligence implementations:

- Reviewing whether given AI features exhibit signs of unequal treatment of various groups helps to assess bias.
- Determining whether stakeholders could grasp and apply AI-enhanced capabilities in suitable manner.
- Making sure artificial intelligence projects complement company values and consumer expectations helps to guarantee value alignment.
- Finding unanticipated consequences of AI implementations that can call for change is one of the challenges.

Reflective Studies: Ethical Gap Analysis

Retrospectives can comprise methodical analysis of ethical AI approaches:

Ethical Debt Assessment: Finding places where haste or another goal impacted ethical considerations.

Process Improvement: Based on experience and results, refining responsible AI techniques

Training Needs: Finding areas where team members require more responsible artificial intelligence knowledge or abilities is training needs.

Stakeholder Feedback: Including outside comments regarding the ethical aspects of team artificial intelligence projects helps stakeholders.

Definition of Done: Ethical Checkpoints

Explicit responsible artificial intelligence requirements should be included of the definition of done:

- "Model explainability documentation completed"
- "Bias testing done across pertinent demographic groups"
- "Completed privacy impact assessment"
- "Responsible AI Owner review performed"
- “Systems of monitoring and alerting applied”

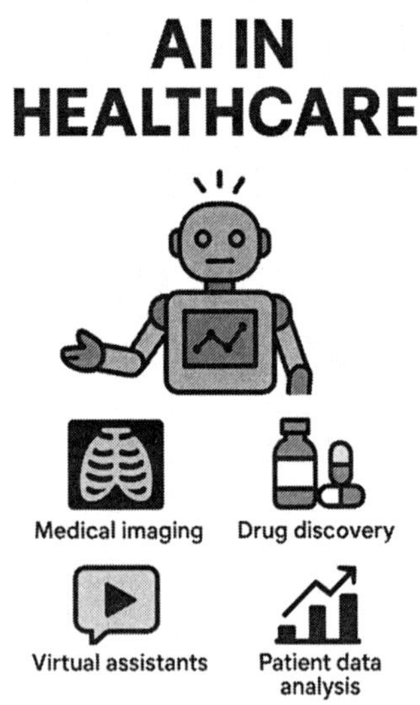

Real-World Implementation: Healthcare AI Case Study

One outstanding illustration of how responsible artificial intelligence may be used into Agile processes comes from a healthcare startup creating AI-powered patient triage solutions.

The difficulty: Using patient symptoms and medical history, the startup's artificial intelligence algorithm advised therapy urgency levels. Early iterations of the system revealed alarming trends of prejudice, with varying advice for patients depending on ethnicity, age, and insurance status instead of only medical considerations.

Agile Integration of Conscious AI

Sprint 1-2: Foundation Setting

- Added to the backlog ethical user stories.
- Created a post of Responsible AI Owner.
- Designed first methods of bias testing.
- Apply fundamental model explainability tools.

Sprint 3-4: Bias Detection and Reducing Agent

- Designed methodical bias testing for several different demographic groupings.
- Apply monitoring and fairness criteria.
- Designed model cards recording known constraints and training statistics.
- Established human review systems for high-stakes decisions

Sprint 5-6: Openness and explainability

- Designed patient-friendly AI recommendations' explanations.
- Designed clinician dashboards illustrating artificial intelligence thinking.
- Put in place systems for contesting AI decisions.
- Created audit paths for every AI-inspired choice.

Sprint 7-8: Keeping Watch and Constant Improvement

- Applied production monitoring for performance and bias.
- Designed automated alarms for odd AI behaviour.
- Developed consistent bias auditing policies
- Use feedback loops to always enhance your models.

Results and Effect

After eight sprints of prudent AI integration:

- Over racial categories, bias measurements rose by 73%; over age groupings, by 68%.
- In every target market the solution attained compliance with healthcare AI rules.
- Rising trust in AI recommendations drove 45% increase in clinical acceptance of healthcare providers.
- More consistent and understandable treatment

recommendations help to raise patient satisfaction levels.

- Better knowledge and control helped the development team trust in their AI systems to rise dramatically.

Roles in Responsible AI: Changing Agile Team Structured

Implementing responsible artificial intelligence successfully calls for specialist knowledge inside Agile teams and unambiguous responsibility.

Improved Old Roles

Product Owner Evolution: Beyond conventional prioritizing, Product Owners must now balance ethical considerations with economic value to guarantee that responsible AI features get suitable priority and that AI implementations match customer values and rights.

Scrum Master Enhancement: Scrum Masters help Agile ceremonies to include ethical checkpoints, therefore ensuring that responsible AI issues are regularly addressed without overloading team processes.

Developer Expansion: Core technical competencies for developers must be literacy in responsible artificial intelligence methods, bias testing, explainability tools, and monitoring systems.

Novel Specialized Roles

Responsible AI Owner: An owner of responsible artificial intelligence plays a committed role in ethical compliance throughout AI deployments. This individual guarantees that ethical risk analyses are carried out, responsible AI methods are adhered to, and ethical AI issues are first contacted via this person.

AI Ethics Reviewer: Reviewing AI implementations for ethical consequences, doing bias audits, and guaranteeing adherence to pertinent laws and organizational values; a job aimed at AI ethics reviewer, is what I do.

AI Transparency Specialist: Responsible for making sure AI systems offer suitable explanations and that stakeholders grasp AI capabilities and constraints, the AI Transparency Specialist

Methodologies for Responsible AI Application in Practice

Using responsible artificial intelligence calls for certain tools and approaches fit for everyday Agile methods.

Tools for Transparency and Documentation

- Comprehensive documentation of training data sources, collecting techniques, recognized biases, and constraints under Data Nutrition Labels. These labels enable teams to know what their artificial intelligence systems "learned" and where issues might surface.
- Detailed information of how models were trained, tested, and validated including performance across many groups, planned use cases, and known constraints.
- Complete description of AI system design, decision-making procedures, and human supervision systems.

Testing Strategies and Assessment Tools

- Helping teams prioritize responsible AI initiatives by means of a methodical framework for assessing AI implementations depending on possible impact and probability of ethical issues.
- Standardized methods for evaluating AI outputs across pertinent demographic and contextual categories are called bias testing protocols.
- Technical execution of fairness measures suitable for certain AI applications and environments is ensured here.

Monitoring and Incident Reaction

- Real-time monitoring of AI system performance including bias measures, accuracy across many groups, and anomalous behaviour identification using artificial intelligence performance dashboards
- Structured procedures for recording, investigating, and handling AI-related events or inadvertent results comprise incident reporting systems.
- Mechanisms for gathering and integrating stakeholder comments on AI system performance and impact constitute feedback integration systems.

Mechanisms of Governance and Inspection

- Cross-functional teams in charge of verifying ethical compliance and reviewing high-risk AI projects are AI Review Boards.
- Clear procedures for handling ethical issues or artificial intelligence system faults discovered during production or development use help to ensure this.
- Systematic evaluations of AI applications help to guarantee continuous compliance with ethical guidelines and legal criteria.

Main Learnings

As we draw to an end our investigation of responsible artificial intelligence in Agile environments, a number of important realizations surface:

- Responsible artificial intelligence is not optional; rather, it is a necessary component of sustainable artificial intelligence deployment that guards society, users, and businesses against the hazards of unbridled AI deployment.
- Through their iterative procedures, cooperative culture, and emphasis on ongoing development, agile teams are especially positioned to operationalize ethical artificial intelligence.
- Early and frequent embedding of ethical issues helps to turn ethics from a compliance burden into a natural component of delivery culture, therefore enabling responsible artificial intelligence to be a natural aspect of team working rather than a restraint from without.
- The fast-changing regulatory environment calls for Agile teams to create adaptive responsible AI solutions that can grow with shifting needs and expectations.
- By fostering trust, raising decision quality, and lowering risks that can compromise long-term performance, responsible artificial intelligence improves rather than compromises team effectiveness.

- Responsible artificial intelligence depends on cross-functional collaboration, which calls for new roles, improved abilities, and methodical incorporation of ethical issues into technical development processes.

Building on the trust foundation formed by responsible AI practices to improve team well-being and performance, our next chapter will examine how artificial intelligence may assist construct psychologically secure and emotionally aware Agile teams.

CHAPTER 7:

Safe Teans, Strong Teams – Tracking Mood aid Mindset with AI

7

SAFE TEAMS, STRONG TEAMS

TRACKING MOOD AND MINDSET WITH AI

INTRODUCTION: BEYOND PRODUCTIVITY METRICS

During their Monday morning stand-up, Sarah noted something was odd. On paper, the team's speed seemed fantastic; they were reaching their sprint targets and providing features on time. Usually their most vocal member, Jake, had been providing shorter updates recently. Maria appeared less interested in retrospectives. And the general vitality of their online conferences felt... varied.

Conventional Agile measurements failed to reflect what Sarah felt. Cycle times, burndown charts, and story points finished all seemed good. Still, the team dynamics didn't seem right. Many Agile teams today deal with this gap: we have grown quite good at quantifying what gets done, but we find it difficult to gauge people's feelings during that process.

Effective Agile teams are psychologically safe as well as highly productive. Innovation blossoms when team members feel free to be honest, take calculated chances, and speak up. People forward audacious concepts. They fast own mistakes. When they need assistance, they ask. Everything else Agile teams aim for starts from this psychological safety.

The difficulty comes in determining something as complex as emotional well-being, though. How can we monitor team health in ways that benefit rather than damage? Here is where artificial intelligence may truly change things; not by substituting human intuition but rather by providing statistics to back up and corroborate what outstanding leaders already sense.

Why Agile Teams Need Psychological Safety

Using hundreds of teams, Google's well-known Project Aristotle investigation sought to identify what factors would make certain groups more successful than others. The top teams were supposed to have either the best resources, the clearest procedures, or the smartest members. Rather, they came onto something simpler and more significant: team efficiency was mostly predicted by psychological safety.

Agile teams especially should pay great attention to this result. Open communication and trust define all we do in Agile.

The Agile-Safety Relationships

Consider Agile fundamental principles:

- Daily stand-ups call for participants to discuss what isn't working and request assistance. Team members that feel unsafe will hide underlying issues and provide surface-level updates.
- Retrospectives only help when people feel free to provide frank comments about mistakes. Retrospectives become polite conversations avoiding the actual problems without safety.
- Realistic approximations and honest capacity conversations define sprint planning. Teams lacking safety will either under-commit to escape responsibility or over-commit to please stakeholders.
- Pair programming and code reviews call for vulnerability; that is, presenting your work to others and embracing comments. These activities turn from learning chances to defensive ones without psychological safety.

What Results When Safety Is Missing?

Agile teams suffer in known patterns when psychological safety is low:

- People avoid offering fresh ideas because they worry about criticism or rejection. The squad starts to turn away risks and settles for small changes.

- Team members conceal issues until they become crises, therefore breaking down transparency. Problems that early intervention may rapidly fix become main obstacles.
- People push themselves past reasonable boundaries when they are unable to communicate tension or ask for support. Because they internalize pressure, high performers sometimes suffer most.
- Good people start seeking for alternative possibilities. Replacing seasoned team members costs much more than just hiring; you also lose institutional knowledge and team cohesion.

Team Health: The Data Behind It

Studies repeatedly highlight the financial value of psychological safety:

- High psychological safety teams are 47% more likely to surpass performance targets.
- Their rates of turnover are 27% lower.
- They produce 67% more ground-breaking ideas.
- From setbacks, they bounce back 43% faster.

Psychological safety especially for Agile teams directly relates with speed, quality, and customer happiness. Safe teams tackle issues early on and support one another, hence they iterate faster.

How Artificial Intelligence Tracks Team Health

Here is where artificial intelligence finds value; not as a substitute for human leadership but rather as an early warning system enabling leaders to spot trends they would overlook.

AI systems can examine communication patterns, behaviour, and language in ways that reveal team emotional wellness. The secret is starting discussions with these realizations rather than passing judgment on individuals.

Language Pattern Study

- By looking at team channel, email, and meeting transcript communications, artificial intelligence can spot changes suggesting stress or disengagement:
- Natural language processing can find whether someone's speech veers toward more formal, aloof, or negative. Usually writing "Thanks for the

help!" a team member may begin to write merely "Thanks" during trying times.

- Artificial intelligence can monitor the varying contributions made by team members to conversations. Usually curious and helpful, someone who asks questions and provides ideas may grow quiet when they're hurting.
- People typically switch their language when under stress. They might grow more categorical ("That won't work") or employ more hedging language ("I think maybe we could...").
- Variations in people's response times to communications can point to degrees of involvement or stress related to job.

Behavioural Pattern Identification

- Beyond language, artificial intelligence can monitor behaviour linked to team health:
- AI can examine who speaks during stand-ups, how long individuals talk, and if team member engagement is evenly distributed.
- Tools can monitor team cohesion indicators including frequency of group projects, help-seeking behaviour, and knowledge sharing; all of which reflect how often individuals cooperate.
- AI can detect when people begin working odd hours, which could point to burnout or stress prior to clear indication.
- Changes in the way people apply development tools, project management systems, or

communication platforms might expose patterns of involvement.

Real-Time Leader Comments

The most useful artificial intelligence systems offer team leaders practical insights rather than only data gathering ability.

Early Warning Alerts: "Jake's communication patterns suggest he might be feeling overwhelmed. Consider checking in with him," early warning alert says.

Team Trends: "Generally team sentiment has been declining for three weeks. This might be a good time for a focused retrospective."

Positive Recognition: "Maria has been especially helpful to other team members this sprint; her collaboration score is at an all-time high."

Intervention Advice: "Based on trends from similar teams, consider adjusting sprint scope or scheduling extra support sessions."

Use Case: Active Mood Tracking

Let us examine how one company effectively included sentiment artificial intelligence into their operations.

The Challenge

Three time zones separated the worldwide product development team TechFlow. They regularly exceeded their delivery targets and followed good Agile techniques. Chen, their manager, observed, nonetheless, minute indicators of team tension in virtual conferences. People looked to be (appeared to be) less involved. Retrosights seemed flat. A few team members had complained of not feeling close to their peers.

Traditional measurements fell short in capturing these issues. Velocity appeared fine. Goals for sprints were being reached. Chen, though, realized the team was not doing well.

AI Integration

The team chose to test sentiment analysis along with their retroactive procedure. They applied an instrument capable of analysing:

- Pre-retroactive anonymous polls conducted in several languages
- Transcripts of meetings from their bi-weekly reviews
- Sentiment of slack messages on their team channels
- Individual reactions to weekly one-on-ones

The artificial intelligence technology produced mood reports suggesting Chen might evaluate before team meetings.

The Discovery

Six weeks of data collecting turned up an obvious trend. Chen had detected something, but the AI showed something else: team morale was dropping steadily over time. The data revealed:

- Sentiment scores overall falling from 7.2 to 5.8 (out of 10).
- Less engagement in team chat conversations
- More project communications using formal language
- Less team member cooperative contacts

The fact that the drop was constant among all team members raised most questions since it indicated a structural problem instead of personal one.

The Response

Equipped with this information, Chen addressed the squad differently than he could have otherwise done. Rather than waiting for issues to develop organically, he aggressively corrected the trends:

Focused Retrospective: Chen encouraged the staff to debate what might be causing the drop after sharing the mood trends; anonymously.

Workload Adjustment: The crew came to see they had been progressively picking up more without considering their capabilities. They chose to cut their next sprint scope by twenty percent.

Connection Time: They included fifteen minutes of social time before their sprint planning meetings and optional "coffee chat" sessions for casual chatting.

Individual Check-ins: Chen set up one-on-one meetings with every team member to learn about their particular worries and experiences.

The Results

The effect was quantifiable and ongoing:

- Sentiment ratings came back to 7.5 in a month.
- From 78% to 91% the rates of sprint completion improved.
- Team members said they felt closer to one another.
- Retrospective involvement become more honest and engaged.
- Two team members who had been considering quitting chose to stay.

The important realization was that the AI did not fix their problems; rather, it alerted them to problems before they developed into crises.

AI-Enabled Team Wellness Tools

Agile teams now have several instruments to monitor and raise psychological safety:

Platform for Team Engagement

- OfficeVibe offers anonymous pulse surveys and participation counts. Over time teams can monitor mood, work satisfaction, and comments on management techniques.

- Culture Amp provides action planning tools and more thorough engagement surveys with benchmarking data.
- 15Five mixes weekly check-ins with goal tracking and peer recognition tools.

Methods of Communication Analysis

- Humanise studies patterns of workplace interaction to determine the degree of cooperation and spot any relationship problems.
- Tracking attention time, meeting patterns, and teamwork practices helps Microsoft Viva Insights find stress indicators and problems with work-life balance.
- Glint: Based on many feedback sources, offers real-time employee sentiment analysis.

Agile Tools for Specialized Needs

- Team Retro with AI Plugins improves retrospectives via sentiment analysis, mood tracking, and anonymous feedback aggregation.
- ScrumGenius comprises team health dashboards and mood tracking tools and stand-up automation.
- AI-powered study of team collaboration behaviors during virtual whiteboarding sessions creates miro mood boards.

Specialized Integration Solutions

Many teams create unique solutions by combining artificial intelligence APIs with current instruments:

- Sentiment analysis of Slack chats made with Google Cloud Natural Language API
- Microsoft Teams for meeting analysis connected with Azure Cognitive Services
- Jira plugins tracking team sentiment alongside project statistics

Ethical Issues: Making Responsible Use of AI

Enormous responsibility accompanies enormous power. Starting to monitor team emotions and actions calls for great caution on how you gather, evaluate, and apply that data.

Explicit Consent Is Crucially Important

Team members have to agree to any monitoring and understand it.

- Clearly state exactly the information you are gathering and the intended use for it.
- Use an opt-in rather than a required approach for involvement.
- Ask team members routinely whether they feel comfortable with the monitoring.
- Simple ways for people to opt out without penalty would help with easy exit.

Maintain data anonymity and aggregation

One has to guard personal privacy:

- Using AI insights helps one to grasp team trends rather than evaluating individual performance.
- Aggregate Reporting: Show team trends instead of individual scores from present data.
- Data Minimization: Just gather information truly required for team health analysis.
- Restricted access to detailed AI analysis outputs

Help rather than surveillance

Helping teams comes first, not watching over them:

- Focus of coaching: start encouraging dialogues based on insights instead of performance management talks.
- Team ownership lets teams view their own data and make decisions about how to react.
- Present artificial intelligence insights as team health data rather than performance assessment using positive framing.
- Human judgment calls for always combining artificial intelligence insights with human intuition and direct communication.

Openness and Authority

Teams must grasp and manage their artificial intelligence systems:

- Use AI technologies that can explain how they arrive at decisions whenever at all practicable.
- Data portability means teams should be able to view and export their own data.
- Review often to see whether the AI monitoring is really improving things.
- Teams should be able to cease AI monitoring depending on their requirements or change it.

Optimal Approaches for Execution

Effective integration of artificial intelligence into team wellness calls for careful change management and continuous awareness of technological as well as human aspects.

Start small and develop trust

- Starting with team members who are eager about the idea and capable of offering helpful criticism, pilot with volunteers.
- Start with one AI wellness tool instead of trying to run all-at once thorough monitoring.
- Share pilot program findings honestly so other teams may observe the value and method of approach.
- Scale AI wellness products depending on proven benefit and team comfort instead of pushing adoption deadlines.

Combine Information with Discussion

AI offers useful facts; human interaction gives background and meaning.

- Rather of substituting AI insights for one-on-one meetings, use them to guide them.
- Share gathered insights with teams and let them decipher the data.
- Always ask people to assist you in deciphering what might be causing the trends AI finds.
- Work with groups to create reactions to AI findings instead than dictating fixes.

Add It to Your Agile DNA.

The most effective applications include wellness artificial intelligence into current Agile methods:

- One input into retrospective conversations should be team health data.
- Add short team wellness exams to sprint planning or review ceremonies.
- Establish team health standards alongside definitions of done for user stories.
- Agile and Scrum Masters should be trained to apply AI wellness insights.

Monitor the Monitoring

Track whether your AI wellness products are really improving things:

- Ask team members whether they value the tools and why.
- Track whether teams equipped with AI wellness technologies exhibit improved performance, retention, or engagement.
- Review and change your strategy often in line with what you discover.
- Track whether artificial intelligence tools are producing the culture you desire or having unanticipated consequences.

Important Lessons

As we draw to a close our investigation of team wellness driven by artificial intelligence, a few particularly noteworthy revelations surface:

- Agile success starts with psychological safety. Without it, every other tool and technique we use would perform less than ideal. Teams must feel comfortable if they are to be open, take calculated chances, and work successfully together.
- Only in ethical use will artificial intelligence highlight trends people overlook. These instruments should improve human leadership, not substitute it. Starting better interactions is the aim; emotional management is not to be automated.
- Translation of artificial intelligence findings into supporting team actions depends critically on Scrum Masters and Agile trainers. They require emotional intelligence to act on such insights

effectively as well as technical knowledge of what AI tools can offer.

- Strong teams are safe, supported, self-aware rather than merely quick. Teams that invest in team health with technical competencies are those who regularly produce outstanding performance over time.
- Implementation calls for equal attention to change management as to technology. The most advanced artificial intelligence systems will fail if teams mistrust them or lack knowledge about how to apply insights for good.

It's time to consider more broadly now that we have seen how artificial intelligence may support the success of specific teams. In our next chapter, we will look at how companies might build the systems, governance, and culture required to scale Agile methods driven by artificial intelligence across whole businesses. We will examine transformation offices, change management techniques, and leadership styles that enable AI + Agile to be used at organizational scale.

Chapter 8:
The Agile+AI Transformation Office
Enabling Enterprise-Wide Synergy

8

CREATING AGILE+AI TRANSFORMATION OFFICE

INTRODUCTION: THE EVOLUTION OF ENTERPRISE GUIDANCE

In late 2024, a Fortune 500 financial institution was confronted with a challenge that would soon become ubiquitous across industries. They had piloted AI-amped Agile practices in three product teams with great success, realizing significant gains in sprint velocity and customer satisfaction. But as news spread and interest increased, they realized a new problem: chaos.

Various departments were embracing conflicting AI technologies. Experimental AI copilots were being aggressively developed by some teams while others were holding back on data privacy. The legal team was falling behind with their ability to meet responsible AI standards in various projects. Worst of all, the positive outcomes from their pilots weren't translating at scale.

The answer wasn't more tech; it was more orchestration. They required what we today know as an Agile+AI Transformation Office: a purpose-driven nerve center that could lead, govern, and speed the convergence of AI and Agile ways of working throughout the enterpris

What Is the Agile+AI Transformation Office?

The Agile+AI Transformation Office is a next-generation PMO and Agile Center of Excellence. Different from its ancestors, which were based primarily on process standardization or tool deployment, this office tackles the special challenges of complexity that result from intelligent systems and adaptive methodologies.

Fundamentally, the Agile+AI Transformation Office is:

- **Strategic Orchestrator:** Aligning AI initiatives with business value streams and Agile delivery frameworks
- **Capability Builder:** Building organization competency in AI-fortified Agile practices
- **Governance Guardian:** Embedding responsible AI practices into Agile processes
- **Innovation Catalyst:** Driving the deployment of successful AI+Agile patterns and encouraging experimentation

Why Traditional Approaches Fall Short

Traditional PMOs tend to struggle with AI+Agile projects since they were built for linear, predictable projects. The conventional Agile CoEs concentrate on process adoption but do not necessarily have the required technical expertise for AI governance. The Agile+AI Transformation Office fills in these gaps as it realizes that:

AI Projects Are Experimentation-Driven by Nature: Contrary to traditional software features, AI projects entice hypothesis testing, model validation, and iteration improvement cycles that cannot be accommodated in regular project templates.

Cross-Functional Collaboration Is Key: Effective AI+Agile adoption demands smooth cooperation among data scientists, engineers, product owners, and ethics experts; a degree of integration silos are unable to facilitate.

Governance Must be Dynamic: Ethical AI practices must adapt to regulation updates, technological innovation, and organizational insight; calling for governance mechanisms that are themselves agile.

Core Roles of the Transformation Office

1. Strategic Alignment and Portfolio Management

The office has a single, comprehensive perspective of all AI+Agile work throughout the organization to ensure alignment with business strategy and de-duplication. This consists of:

- **AI Initiative Mapping:** Listing all AI pilots, experiments, and scaled production across teams
- **Value Stream Integration**: Integrating AI capabilities to customer value delivery and business results

- **Resource Optimization:** Aligning shared AI infrastructure, talent, and budgeting
- **Success Pattern Identification:** Identifying and scaling the most effective AI+Agile combinations

2. Capability Development and Enablement

Establishing organizational competency through systematic investment in people, processes, and platforms:

- **Competency Framework Development:** Defining the levels of AI literacy for various Agile roles (Product Owner, Scrum Master, Developer, Tester)
- **Training Program Curation**: Curating learning paths that integrate AI basics with Agile practice improvement
- **Coaching Network Expansion:** Upskilling current Agile coaches to assist AI-enabled teams
- **Community Building**: Creating communities of practice where teams may exchange AI+Agile learnings

3. Governance and Risk Management

The office makes sure AI integration upholds instead of dilutes organizational values and compliance obligations:

- **Responsible AI Framework:** Creating ethical standards, bias testing protocols, and explainability measures

- **Compliance Monitoring:** Monitoring compliance with regulations such as the EU AI Act, GDPR, and industry-specific regulations
- **Risk Assessment:** Assessing the potential effects of AI implementations on team dynamics, customer experience, and business operations
- **Incident Response:** Developing processes for handling AI-related issues or ethical concerns

4. Tooling and Platform Strategy

Aligning the technology ecosystem to accommodate AI+Agile practices:

- **Tool Evaluation and Selection:** Assembling AI copilots, analytics platforms, and integration solutions
- **Platform Integration:** Enabling AI tools to integrate smoothly with current Agile toolchains (Jira, GitHub, Confluence)
- **Data Pipeline Enablement:** Enabling teams to have quality data at their disposal for AI projects
- **Security and Privacy:** Enforcing data governance practices that safeguard sensitive data

Organizational Structure and Roles

The Transformation Office Team

AI+Agile Transformation Lead: An executive who gets both domains and can exert influence across business units.

This individual is the main face of the transformation office vis-à-vis executive leadership.

Responsible AI Officer: Deliberately deals with ethical AI behavior, compliance, and risk management. They guarantee that all AI+Agile projects fulfill organizational values as well as regulatory specifications.

Technical Enablement Manager: Facilitates the connection between AI capabilities and Agile methodologies and supports teams in learning how to best incorporate AI tools into their processes.

Change Management Specialist: Assists organizational uptake by means of communication, training, and cultural change programs.

Data and Analytics Architect: Provides teams with access to the data infrastructure and analytics capabilities required for AI projects.

Embedded Partnership Model

In contrast to working as a distinct organization, the most effective transformation offices place partners directly within business units:

- **Transformation Partners:** Seasoned practitioners who collaborate with teams to execute AI+Agile practices
- **AI Ethics Ambassadors:** Experts who assist teams in understanding responsible AI considerations within their unique context

- **Technical Advisors:** AI tool selection, implementation, and optimization experts who offer guidance

Implementation Roadmap

Phase 1: Foundation (Months 1-3)

- Stand up the transformation office team and governance structure
- Organizational assessment of existing AI and Agile maturity
- Define responsible AI framework and compliance requirements
- Develop initial tooling standards and selection criteria

Phase 2: Pilot and Learn (Months 4-9)

- Collaborate with 3-5 high-potential teams to apply AI+Agile practices
- Create early training content and coaching materials
- Define measurement structures for monitoring success
- Develop templates and playbooks from pilot learnings

Phase 3: Scale and Optimize (Months 10-18)

- Scale support to more teams based on pilot success
- Iterate governance processes based on practical experience
- Develop community of practice networks
- Optimize tools and processes continually

Phase 4: Institutionalize (Months 19+)

- Integrate AI+Agile practices into standard business procedures
- Shift from transformation office to sustained center of excellence
- Emphasis on continuous innovation and emerging tech adoption

Success Metrics and Measurement

The transformation office measures success along various metrics:

Adoption Metrics: Adoption of AI+Agile practices by number of teams, rates of adoption of tools, completion of training

Performance Metrics: Improvement in sprint velocity, quality, and time-to-market acceleration

Maturity Metrics: Progress of the organization through the Crawl-Walk-Run-Fly model

Ethical Metrics: Compliance with Responsible AI scores, detection and mitigation of bias rates, transparency measurements

Innovation Measures: Number of new AI+Agile patterns established, cross-team knowledge sharing, experimental success rates

Real-World Success Story

One multinational manufacturing company set up their Agile+AI Transformation Office for end-to-end digital transformation management across 15 business units. In 18 months, they realized:

- 40% project duplication reduction through improved coordination
- 35% increase in sprint velocity across AI-improved teams
- 95% responsible AI guideline compliance rate
- 60% rise in cross-functional collaboration score
- $12M in quantified business value from AI+Agile projects

The secret to their success was viewing the transformation office not as a governing body, but as a service organization committed to supporting team success.

Key Takeaways

The Agile+AI Transformation Office represents a new model for enterprise guidance; one that embraces experimentation while ensuring responsible implementation. By focusing on enablement rather than control, these offices can accelerate organizational adoption of AI+Agile practices while maintaining the human-centered values that make Agile successful.

Succeeding necessitates meticulous attention to technical competencies as well as organizational change management. The best transformation offices balance strategic thinking with hands-on support for implementation, an environment where AI augments instead of diminishing human judgment and co-operation.

While organizations increasingly develop their strategy for AI+Agile integration, the transformation office will continue to be a vital piece of the puzzle; evolving its own methodology to address new challenges but always keeping its central purpose in mind: facilitating intelligent, adaptive, and ethical styles of work.

In our following chapter, we will see how AI is transforming planning and prediction in supply chains, vendor relationships, and operational decision-making, taking Agile thinking beyond software development into the operational core of today's businesses.

Chapter 9: Intelligent Planning – AI in Supply Chains, Vendors, & Forecasting

Adoring and illuraiton ehlolof a Exprescing supply olationconchip and AI In suaple ons oniimps Forecasting

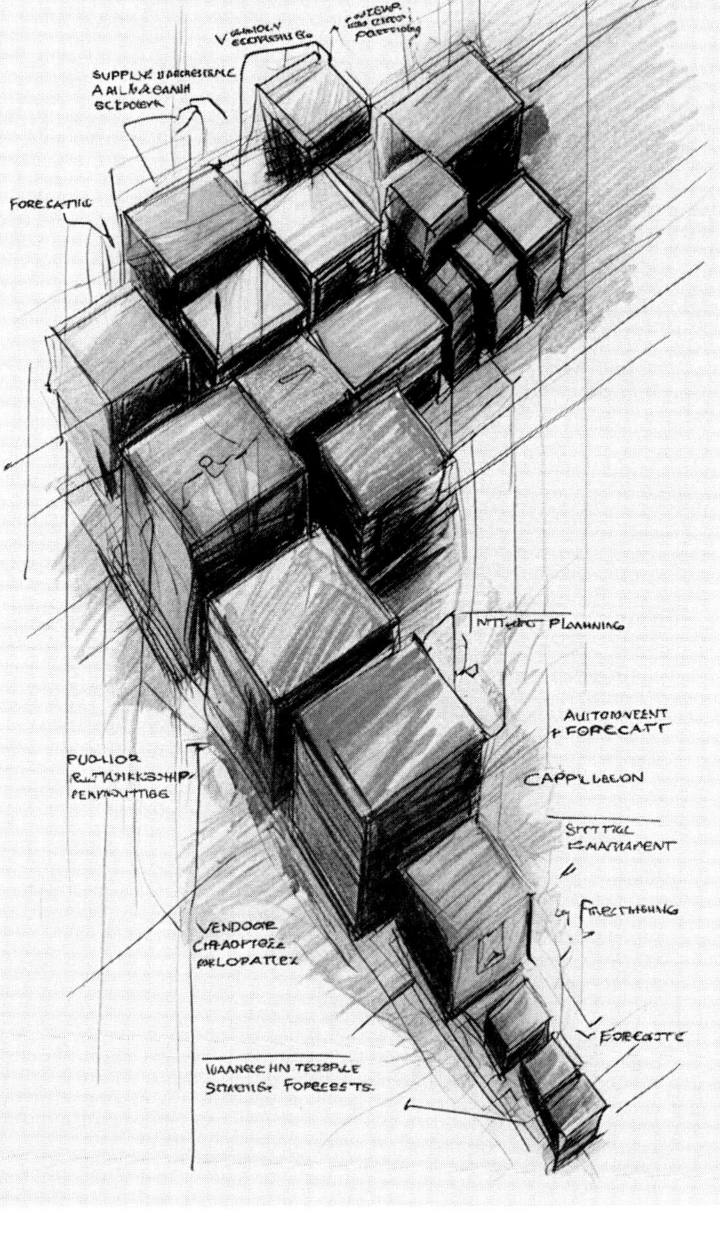

9

USING AI IN SUPPLY CHAINS, VENDORS, AND FORECASTING TO PLAN BETTER

INTRODUCTION: WHEN THE UNEXPECTED BECOMES EXPECTED

The Suez Canal was blocked again on March 23, 2024, by the Ever Given container ship. But this time, something amazing happened at Global Consumer Electronics (GCE), a Fortune 100 company that had learnt the hard way how to deal with supply chain challenges in the past. Their AI-powered planning system had already located 847 shipments that were disrupted, thought out different routes to get them to their destination, and begun talking to backup suppliers through their autonomous negotiation platform within six hours of the blockage.

More importantly, their Agile planning teams didn't panic or have extended crisis meetings. Instead, they regarded the disruption as just another piece of knowledge to help them get ready for the sprint. They swiftly ran through a number of scenarios, tested out several solutions, and adjusted their plan based on what they saw happening in real time. What could have led to weeks of reactive firefighting became a planned, rational response that actually made their supply chain stronger.

This is a huge difference in how modern firms prepare. Instead of completing static, yearly exercises, they now use dynamic, AI-enhanced Agile procedures that perceive uncertainty as a good thing, not a bad one.

Planning's Evolution: From Prediction to Adaptation

The premise behind traditional planning is that we can make quite good guesses about what will happen in the future. Supply chain managers generate accurate forecasts, procurement teams write annual contracts, and operations teams figure out how much capacity they will need based on what has happened in the past. In situations that were steady and predictable, this strategy performed quite well.

From the business world today, nothing is stable. Changes in the weather that have never happened before are happening because of climate change. Changes in geopolitics can affect trade routes overnight. People's tastes change frequently on social media. You wouldn't think that technology would originate from locations like this. In this case, it is more vital to be able to change quickly than to be able to make accurate predictions.

Where AI and Agile Meet in Planning

AI is good at finding patterns, developing models of varied circumstances, and digesting a lot of real-time data. Agile methods are great for making decisions as a group, fast going through the process of making changes, and adapting to change. They create something altogether unique when utilised together in planning: intelligent adaptability.

AI lets machines feel things: machine learning models that can pick up on early indicators of changes in demand, supply difficulties, or market developments before they are obvious to human analysts.

Agile lets you respond rapidly because cross-functional teams can quickly look at options, test solutions, and make changes without having to wait for long approval processes. They work together to assist organisations move from being reactive to being proactive.

Using AI-Agile Practices to Change Demand Forecasting

Traditional demand forecasting relies heavily on historical sales data and seasonal trends. These are still important inputs, but AI-enhanced forecasting uses hundreds of other signals, like the mood on social media, the weather, economic indicators, how competitors act, and even satellite photos of retail parking lots.

Agile planning teams produce a number of projections based on different scenarios and update them with fresh information. This is not the same as making one "golden forecast" that everyone has to follow.

Daily Stand-ups for Planners: Demand planners now meet every day to speak about changes to the forecast, seek for new signals, and collaborate with the marketing and supply chain teams. AI offers the facts, and people decide what to do with them and what they mean. **Forecast Cycles Based on Sprints**: Instead of changing their forecasts every month or three months, teams work in two-week sprints. This helps them use new data and update their assumptions much more quickly.

Example from Real Life: A significant company that creates consumer packaged goods transformed how they get ready for demand by using AI-powered signal detection and Agile planning cycles. They were 23% better at making accurate predictions, but more importantly, they were 60% better at reacting to rapid changes in demand. During the 2024 Olympic Games, they were able to immediately adjust how they sold their items based on AI-analyzed social media and search habits. This helped them sell 40% more in the marketplaces of the host city.

The Pactum AI Revolution: Vendors working together on their own

One of the most exciting aspects about AI-enhanced planning is that platforms for autonomous negotiation and vendor collaboration are becoming more popular. This is a major step forward for Pactum AI. It enables businesses talk to thousands of suppliers at once while still retaining the spirit of collaboration that makes Agile work.

How Pactum AI Works in Agile Environments

Pactum AI doesn't take the place of people who work in procurement. Instead, it works as a smart negotiation assistant that can manage simple vendor transactions and pass on more difficult choices to people. The platform uses natural language processing to understand what providers are saying, machine learning to figure out the best ways to bargain, and game theory to come up with solutions that work for both sides.

Working with Agile Planning Cycles: AI handles the execution of vendor agreements, while human teams make strategic decisions and keep relationships in order. Every day, there are stand-ups to talk about how talks are going, and retrospectives help teams work better with AI partners.

Sprint Reviews with Suppliers: Some businesses now use their AI negotiating platform as a "team member" during sprint reviews. It illustrates the results of negotiations and gives tips on how to make the next cycle better.

Case Study: A global electronics business used Pactum AI to maintain track of its relationships with over 3,000 suppliers. They included the platform to their Agile planning cycles, which lowered the time it took to buy things by 45% and boosted supplier satisfaction scores by 30%. The essential point is that approaching AI like a collaborator instead of a tool helped everyone.

Planning smartly to make the supply chain more resilient

Supply chains are more complex and less stable than they have ever been. Because of climate change, geopolitical tensions, and technology that evolves quickly, there is always trouble. The goal of traditional risk management is to find potential problems and plan what to do if they happen. AI-powered Agile planning takes things a step further by creating systems that can alter and respond quickly to changes as they arise.

Real-Time Risk Detection: AI systems are always watching thousands of signals, such data on port congestion and signs of a supplier's financial health, to detect new threats before they disrupt operations.

Agile Response Teams: When AI systems sense a prospective problem, they instantly establish Agile response procedures. Cross-functional teams may swiftly assess the situation, consider their options, and implement solutions without having to go through protracted approval processes.

Learning All the Time: Every time something goes wrong, you can learn something. Retrospectives help teams find out what worked, what didn't, and how to handle problems better in the future.

The Kinaxis Advantage: Planning at the Same Time

Kinaxis RapidResponse is an example of how supply chain planning software is changing to work with Agile and use AI. Kinaxis lets you plan at the same time for several eventualities. This is not like other planning systems, which need to process in batches and take a long time to update.

Sprint Planning with Scenario Modelling: Planning teams may swiftly try out new ideas, look at the good and bad sides of each one, and make decisions based on the most recent facts. It used to take days to analyse something, but now it can be done in a few hours.

Exception-Based Management: AI systems look for ways to improve things and give them to Agile planning teams to look at. This is different from just managing by exception when problems come up.

Collaborative Decision-Making: The platform helps people from diverse departments work together to make hard planning choices. AI feeds them facts and analysis, and people utilise their judgement and strategic thinking to make decisions.

The Future of Intelligent Operations: Moving Beyond Traditional Planning

As AI and Agile methodologies improve, we are seeing the birth of whole new ways to plan operations:

Digital Twins for Planning: Some companies are constructing digital twins of their whole supply chain. This allows people test out different strategies and situations in a virtual world before they do them in real life.

Autonomous Planning Agents: Advanced AI systems can now make typical planning decisions on their own and only send strange situations to human teams. This allows planners to focus on strategic thinking and relationship management.

Ecosystem-Wide Optimisation: AI-enhanced Instead of just their own businesses or supply chains, agile planning allows companies improve their whole ecosystems. This is good for everyone.

Best Practices for Putting It into Action

Start with Use Cases That Have a Big Effect and Low Risk: Begin implementing AI-enhanced Agile planning in domains where the potential advantages are clear and the risks are minimal. A good place to start is by predicting demand and engaging with suppliers.

Put money into data quality: AI systems only work if they get good data. Before you use AI to help with planning, be sure that the steps for gathering, cleaning, and checking data are good.

Focus on working together with AI: The greatest methods to employ AI see it as a partner, not a replacement. Use the best parts of both people and machines to make things work better.

Embrace Experimentation: Agile planning means being willing to try new things, learn from your failures, and find better ways to do things. Create spaces where people may learn and try things out without being afraid.

Develop Cross-Functional Skills: AI-driven Agile planning requires working together across traditional functional lines. Invest in developing cross-functional teams and capabilities.

Measure and Learn: Set explicit targets for success and verify on a regular basis how well AI-enhanced planning methods are performing. Look back on things to find methods to make them better.

Key Points

AI and Agile methods are coming together to revolutionise how firms make plans and guesses. By combining AI's ability to analyse data with Agile's flexibility to modify, companies can develop planning systems that are both smart and flexible.

You need more than just using new technology to be successful. It entails changing how we think about planning, realising that uncertainty is a constant rather than an exception, and making the organisation robust enough to adapt swiftly to new scenarios.

Companies that know how to use AI to improve Agile planning will have a major advantage over their competitors in a business world that is getting more unstable and difficult. They will be able to spot changes sooner, respond more quickly, and make the most of uncertainty instead of letting it injure them.

Planning for the future isn't about making better assumptions about what will happen next; it's about being able to sensibly change plans when things change. In the next chapter, we'll speak about how these ideas might be used in other areas besides business. They will also work for robots, the Internet of Things, and tests in the real world.

CHAPTER 10: AGILE GETS PHYSICAL – AI IN ROBOTICS, IOT & REAL-WORLD TESTING

10

AGILE GOES PHYSICAL

TESTING IN THE REAL WORLD WITH ROBOTS AND THE INTERNET OF THINGS

INTRODUCTION: THE INTERSECTION OF SOFTWARE AND REALITY

Boston Dynamics engineers were nervous when their latest humanoid robot, Atlas, attempted to navigate an obstacle course in a pristine lab.

But this was no routine robot showcase. The team's third "sprint demo" for the month occurred. They were demonstrating modest changes to Atlas's balance algorithms to a group of individuals representing other departments, such as engineers, product managers, safety specialists, and even customers. The team learned a new trick every two weeks, such as paying more attention to their environments, moving objects better, or climbing stairs more effectively.

The team didn't interpret Atlas's fall as failure; they interpreted it as good intel for the next sprint planning session. The sensors on the robot had collected hundreds of data points about the fall. They would apply this information to inform their AI algorithms about what to do next and improve the story. This problem indicates that how things are made has transformed significantly.

First, individuals used agile techniques to develop software, but now they're applying them to create new concepts for robotics, IoT devices, smart manufacturing, and physical systems where the risk is higher, the feedback cycles are longer, and it is more difficult to solve integration issues.
Why Agile and AI Matter to Things You Can Touch

The waterfall method has been used for a long time to make hardware. Planning, developing, building prototypes, testing them, and finally making the product takes a lot of time. When it was hard and costly to make changes, it made sense. But the things we buy now are getting smarter, more connected, and more dependent on software.

Bots are no longer devices; they are now platforms that learn and become better with AI.

Smartphones, tablets, and other Internet of Things (IoT) gadgets possess heavy software to cooperate with sensors, networks, and edge computing.

Smart production systems use digital twins and foreknowledge analysis to connect physical behaviors. Physical-digital systems cooperate well with Agile's iterative approach and AI's capability to learn. Some of the following are some of the challenges that are unique to this scenario: Longer Feedback Cycles: It is time-consuming to produce and test physical prototypes, but you can change software right away. More at stake: If the program contains a bug, an application may fail. If the robots malfunction, someone is injured.

Difficult Integration: In physical systems, mechanical, electrical, and software components all need to work together.

Regulatory Compliance: Real things need to comply with many rules related to safety and other factors.

Supply Chain Dependencies: You require actual parts with their respective regulations and delivery schedules to make hardware.

Bio-Inspired Robotics: Learning from Nature's Adaptations

Some of the most sophisticated robotics research currently underway is founded on living organisms. It's fascinating the way nature operates according to laws that are quite akin to how Agile development operates. MIT has turtle-like robots and worm-like robots, the former able to move through turbulent water and the latter able to penetrate into small spaces.

These development hardware projects are illustrations of how Agile functions:

Iterative Design: The latest robot generation that is bio-inspired learns from each previous one. Engineers monitor the robot as it operates to observe how it could fail. They also brainstorm how to improve it for the next time.

Cross-Functional Collaboration: Biologists, mechanical engineers, software developers, and AI experts alike must collaborate to make bio-inspired robotics a reality, the same way Agile software teams do.

Continuous Learning: AI algorithms examine the movement data of each test session, look for patterns, and propose changes that will improve the next development iteration.

Minimum Viable Product: Teams do not attempt to copy all about how living organisms move simultaneously. Rather, they begin with essential abilities such as seeing, moving, or grasping and add more along the way.

Real-world example: The MIT soft robotics group created a robot resembling an elephant trunk by producing rapid sprints.

The crew spent every other week on one of three activities: picking up objects of all sizes, navigating around objects that were in their path, or assembling a multitude of parts.

The team utilized AI in order to view movement data and plan out their sprints.

They utilized retrospectives with other department colleagues in order to improve their bio-mechanical concepts. Smart Manufacturing: The Factory as a Team That Can Change China's initial application of humanoid robots in the factory is more than mere automation; it's an entirely different method for production systems to learn and get better. These are not the same robotic gadgets repeating the same action ad infinitum. They are systems that use AI to learn, adapt to new situations, and even collaborate with humans. The Fundamentals of Agile

Manufacturing: Production Planning in Sprints: There are no fixed times to produce things in intelligent factories. They plan in short cycles that can be revised if the demand alters, there are issues with the supply, or there are issues with the quality.

Continuous Integration: Intelligent manufacturing systems, like software CI/CD pipelines, introduce new features to robot behaviors, quality algorithms, and methods to enhance production efficiency on a continuous basis.

Cross-Functional Factory Teams: Factory teams that produce things now have more than managers and operators. They now include data scientists who examine production data, AI specialists who cause robots to improve, and product managers who ensure the plant can satisfy the customer.

Real-Time Retrospectives: Factory workers conduct retrospectives constantly, but AI analysis of production metrics, quality data, and worker feedback assists them in identifying improvements to make.

Case Study: A Shenzhen electronics producer used Agile concepts to develop a smart factory. Humanoid robots learned new assembly tasks each week by observing and performing them. They were able to reconfigure the facility within a few days rather than weeks to improve it for new products, and it remained up to standards of quality and efficiency.

IoT and Edge AI: Fast in the Era of Connected Things

The Internet of Things is one of the most complex areas where virtual and real systems collide. Smart home devices, wearable devices, industrial sensors, intelligent autos, and intelligent home devices all have physical components and clever software that must function in the real world, which isn't always simple to presume.

Edge AI Challenges: Edge devices must be capable of making intelligent decisions even if they lack much processing power, the internet is slow, or they are in different locations. This differs from AI systems that operate in the cloud. Agile practices can assist with some special challenges that arise during development.

Patterns for Developing IoT in an Agile Fashion:

Device-to-Cloud Feedback Loops: IoT devices always know exactly what they're doing. This informs individuals about what to do next and how to behave in the moment. This informs teams about which features are most critical to customers as they schedule a sprint.

Over-the-Air Iteration: More recent IoT devices are able to download software upgrades wirelessly.

This allows Agile teams to make changes in a hurry and receive feedback from actual users.

Federated Learning: AI models can be trained from data in thousands of devices that are being used already without compromising people's privacy.

This allows Agile teams to experiment with their product in so many different ways.

Digital Twin Integration: Digital twins are linked to actual IoT devices so new features can be tested and prototyped instantly before being utilized.

Applying it in the real world:

A smart thermostat firm utilized both Agile and AI to enhance their products.

Every sprint was based on a particular customer need, such as saving energy, achieving comfort in the home, or using other smart home systems.

Agile teams made their AI algorithms quickly test and update, which considered the usage of millions of devices.

The energy savings were 25% higher than anticipated, and customer satisfaction improved by 40%.

How to deal with limits in life

Simulation-First Development: Powerful simulation environments enable Agile teams to quickly experiment with concepts before making physical prototypes. You can experiment safely with virtual reality, physics engines, and digital twins.

Modular Hardware Architecture: Modular designs facilitate quicker assembly of things. You can modify one piece at a time, which simplifies the process of making changes and makes it faster to create new versions.

Continuous Testing Infrastructure: Automated testing frameworks that can execute physical tests continuously, collect data, and identify faults autonomously.

Iteration of Safety First: Proper safety regulations ensure that Agile iteration does not compromise safety. We do safety checks at the end of every sprint, and retrospectives are a matter of what did we learn about safety and how do we improve.

Things and tools that make it easier to do physical agile work

ROS (Robot Operating System): This is a set of software tools that allows you to apply Agile methodologies to create apps for robots.

You can use model-based design methodologies to build and test things again and again with MATLAB and Simulink.

You can now utilize Unity and Unreal Engine to build digital twins and robots that resemble you.

With Kubernetes and Docker, you are able to execute the same application on different types of hardware.

Platforms for Edge AI such as NVIDIA Jetson, Intel Movidius, among others allow AI to execute on devices that are not very powerful.

Best Methods of Using Agile Development in the Real World

Embrace Simulation: Leverage digital twins and simulated environments to learn quicker and make changes at a lower cost.

Design for Modularity: Design hardware and software that allows you to swap or augment parts of the system without necessarily altering everything.

Invest in testing infrastructure: Automated testing is much more critical for real things than for software.

Plan Safety: Safety needs to be part of each step in Agile development, not an afterthought.

Create Cross-Functional Teams: When producing things from wood or metal, individuals from disparate domains must collaborate more than when producing software.

Key Points

When we apply Agile and AI concepts to create real things, it assists us in creating things that perform better in the real world. Agile's iterative approach and AI's learnability can empower teams create smarter, more adaptable physical things that serve the purposes of their clients.

You must redirect the manner in which you previously believed you could make hardware in order to excel. You will also have to conform to the same safety and reliability standards as physical objects do. Businesses that can find the harmony of this balance will create products that not only serve today's demands but become better and shift with time.

You can't simply create smarter tools for creating things in the future. We must also create intelligent systems that can learn, adapt, and become smarter as they grow.

In the following chapter, we will discuss how blockchain and smart contracts are enabling new types of decentralised Agile collaboration. Ordinary companies cannot do these.

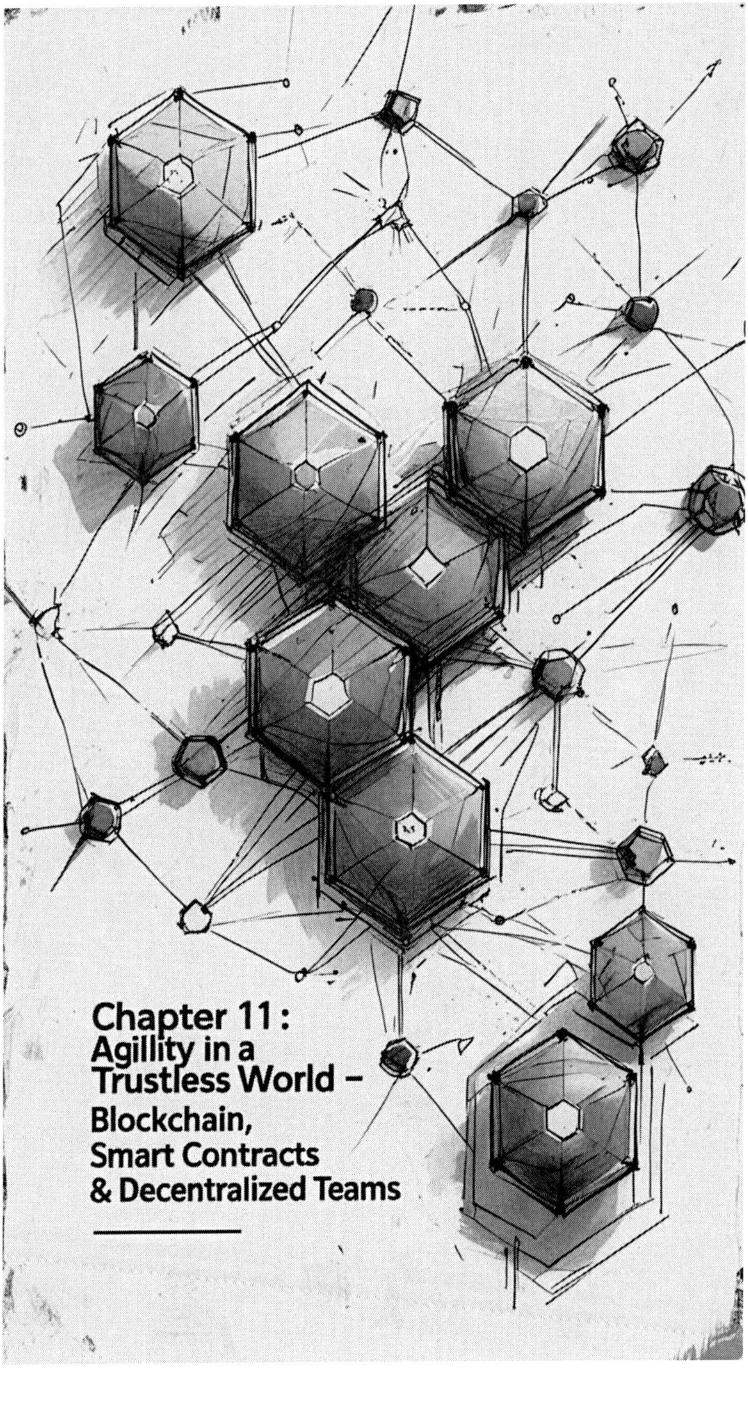

Chapter 11 : Agillity in a Trustless World – Blockchain, Smart Contracts & Decentralized Teams

11

AGILE IN THE AGE OF BLOCKCHAIN & SMART CONTRACTS

INTRODUCTION: TRUST IN A TRUSTLESS WORLD

Early in 2024, something unusual occurred on three continents. A decentralized autonomous organization (DAO) called OpenDev was building an open-source AI platform entirely on blockchain Agile methods. Developers from 47 countries joined sprints with no individual leader, no Scrum Master per se, and no company bureaucracy. Smart contracts processed automatically prioritized backlog, sprint commitments, and contributor rewards through open, algorithmic rules.

When São Paulo machine learning engineer Sarah completed a sophisticated natural language processing capability early, the blockchain automatically released her bonus payment; no approvals, no waiting for payroll processing, no geographical limitations. When the team collectively decided to change their architecture in a retrospective, the decision was logged irretrievably to the blockchain, available as an audit trail for future decisions.

It was greater than an experiment in distributed development; it was a vision for how blockchain technology and smart contracts might restructure Agile collaboration to establish trust, provide transparency, and automate on unprecedented levels.

The Trust Challenge in Modern Agile

Early Agile methods certainly involve some trust and shared context. All members of the team are employees of the same corporation, share the same incentives, and fall under the same authority. But as software development becomes increasingly distributed; between companies, countries, and even organizational types; these assumptions disappear.

Consider the difficulties distributed modern teams face:

Validation of Contributions: How do you even rightfully assess and reward contributions of staff members you have never met, dispersed across time zones whose cultural norms differ?

Accountability of Decisions: When product decisions of consequence are being made in virtual meetings across distributed organizations, how do you ensure there are full records of who decided what and why?

Incentive Alignment: How can you align everyone to the

same goals working for multiple employers, with varying compensation systems, and varying career ambitions?

Intellectual Property Protection: How can you protect creative ideas without hindering the openness that permits Agile collaboration?

Blockchain and smart contracts provide new solutions to these trust issues, making new types of Agile collaboration possible that are not feasible with conventional techniques.

Blockchain Basics for Agile Teams

Prior to examining particular uses, it is helpful to have a sense of what blockchain contributes to Agile practices:

Unalterable Record Keeping: Everything sprint responsibility, story completion, and retrospective choice gets stored permanently and cannot be changed, providing unmatched visibility to team activity.

De-Centralized Consensus: Decisions can be made by teams without the need for central authority through voting mechanisms within smart contracts to enable self-organizing teams in real life.

Automatic Execution: Smart contracts are programmed to execute contracts automatically, pay, and trigger action with the occurrence of stipulated conditions, absent administrative expense and ensuring consistency.

Tokenized Incentives: Blockchain facilitates new means of contributor reward and recognition through tokens that can convey anything from voting power to returns to be shared.

Transparent Governance: Each team governance policy, from the delegation of story points to the retro process, can be coded up transparently so that contributors can see exactly how decisions are being made.

Smart Contracts: Automating Agile Agreements

Smart contracts are probably the most exciting application for blockchain technology on Agile teams. Self-executing contracts that will hold terms on some conditions in place automatically get rid of legacy burdens of project management.

Sprint Commitment Contracts: Teams can use smart contracts to automatically mark stories as done, calculate velocity, and reward proportionate to actual delivery rather than planned effort.

Automating Definition of Done: Intelligent, sophisticated definition of done conditions can be employed in smart contracts so that automatic confirmation of completion is derived from various sources; code commit, test coverage, peer review, and stakeholder sign-off.

Automated Retrospective Action Items: Rather than trust that team members will follow up on retrospective action items, smart contracts can monitor automatically for progress and send gentle reminders or escalations when actions go unaddressed.

Cross-Team Dependencies: Because teams are dependent upon each other, smart contracts can automate handoffs, notify downstream teams in case of a change, and schedule integration.

Real-World Example: Blockchain startup developing a decentralized finance platform used smart contracts to guide their Agile process. Sprint goals were used as smart contracts that, upon completion, automatically released milestone payments to writers. Code gates of quality were enforced through automated testing infused with blockchain verification. The result was 99% sprint goal achievement and full transparency into team performance; all without overhead of manual project management.

Pactum AI: Autonomous Vendor Collaboration

One of the most innovative applications of AI and blockchain in Agile environments is vendor negotiation and management independently. Pactum AI is one such new norm in this regard, where artificial intelligence to negotiate hundreds or thousands of vendors at once and blockchain for transparency and enforceability

How Pactum AI Revolutionizes Vendor Collaboration

Maximized Negotiation: AI-powered agents can negotiate complex agreements with vendors based on market conditions, historical performance, and strategic objectives to achieve maximum outcomes.

Blockchain-Encoded Contracts: Every agreement negotiated is recorded on blockchain, rendering immutable contracts that execute mechanically according to performance targets.

On-the-Fly Performance Monitoring: Smart contracts track vendor performance in real time against agreed levels of service, changing payments or triggering renegotiation automatically at thresholds.

Transparent Audit Trails: All negotiation steps, performance assessment, and payment are recorded transparently, offering unprecendented visibility into vendor relationships.

Smooth Workflow Integration: Vendor negotiations are translated into backlog items that are prioritized, estimated, and tracked like any other user story while AI executes and human teams make strategic decisions.

Case Study: A global manufacturing company integrated Pactum AI with blockchain smart contracts to manage their 500+ supply base. The AI was constantly having micro-negotiations with suppliers, and smart contracts took automatic payments based on delivery performance. Result was 23% reduction in costs, 40% boost in supplier satisfaction score, and elimination of payment disputes; while reducing procurement team workload by 60%.

Decentralized Autonomous Organizations (DAOs) and Agile

DAOs are the ultimate in self-organizing teams; teams that operate based on rules coded within smart contracts rather than top-down, centralized control. DAOs represent a thrilling potential for highly distributed, self-directed team operation for those who do Agile.

DAO-Driven Agile Features

Tokenized Governance: Members are given tokens representing voting authority over team decision-making from sprint planning priorities to adjustments to the retrospective process.

Automatic Rewards: Contributions reward and become recognized automatically through token distribution, eliminating subjective performance reviews.

Transparent Decision Making: Team decisions are recorded on blockchain with total transparency into voting patterns and rationale.

Merit-Based Leadership: Leadership roles can be automatically given out based on history of contributions and peer recognition in place of traditional appointment methods.

Global Talent Access: Teams can source contributors from across the globe with no restrictions based on traditional employment.

Implementation Example: One DAO that was constructing an open-source project management system structured solely on Agile principles. Members were rewarded with governance tokens for the completion of user stories, participation in retrospectives, and helping other members. Token-weighted voting was applied to sprint planning, with the most active members having the most influence when it came to setting priorities. The project exhibited whopping (significant) velocity and quality statistics with complete transparency and fairness in reward distribution to members.

Challenges and Considerations

While blockchain and smart contracts offer potent technologies to Agile teams, they also introduce novel challenges:

Technical Sophistication: Implementing blockchain solutions requires vast technical sophistication that may not exist in traditional Agile teams.

Scalability Limitations: Current blockchain technologies are limited by throughput limitations that may restrict their applicability to large Agile operations.

Regulatory Uncertainty: The legal status of smart contracts and DAO governance structures is uncertain in most jurisdictions.

Energy Consumption: Some blockchain technologies have large environmental profiles that can counter organizational sustainability goals.

Cultural Resistance: Traditional organizations may abhor the transparency and decentralization blockchain enables.

Best Practices for Blockchain-Enabled Agile

Start Small and Learn: Pilot initiatives that investigate specific applications of blockchain rather than large-scale changeover initiatives.

Prioritize High-Value Use Cases: Prioritize cases where

blockchain's unique strengths; transparency, automation, and decentralization; create unambiguous value.

Invest in Education: Train team members on blockchain principles and implications before implementing blockchain-enhanced Agile practices.

Balance Transparency with Privacy: Use private or consortium blockchains where confidential data must be protected while achieving desired transparency.

Evolve with Technology and Regulations: Blockchain technology is changing fast; develop systems that can change with technology change and regulatory landscapes.

Future of Trustless Agile Collaboration

As blockchain technology matures and finds its rightfully available state, we foresee even more sophisticated use in Agile settings:

Cross-Organizational Sprints: Teams from several companies cooperating on shared objectives with blockchain to precisely record input and reward distribution.

AI-Governance: Artificial intelligence infrastructure supporting DAOs in making complex decisions about priority for projects, resources, and process optimization.

Tokenized Innovation: Fresh reward and incentivization paradigms built on blockchain-led token economies that link people's work to the success of the collective.

Global Talent Marketplaces: Places where skilled contributors can participate in Agile teams worldwide, and blockchain ensures fair remuneration and recognition regardless of location.

Key Takeaways

Blockchain and smart contracts hold enormous potential to disseminate trust, transparency, and automation throughout Agile processes. Though emerging, they already enable new levels of collaboration that disseminate Agile values outside organizational silos.

Achieving this entails scrupulous care for opportunity and challenge both, with view to beginning small, ongoing learning, and scaling to more sophisticated uses as technology and organizational capability mature.

Blockchain-Agile union is not merely a matter of technology innovation; it's a vision of how work itself might be transformed to be more open, fair, and world-embracing modes of working together.

In the next chapter, we'll be moving our focus to in-the-trenches deployment, providing you with the tools, templates, and materials you need to initiate your own AI-Agile transformation.

CHAPTER 12:
YOUR AI-AGILE
STARTER,
TEMPLATES, &
TACTICAL ASSETS

12

TOOLS & TEMPLATES

YOUR AI-AGILE STARTER KIT

INTRODUCTION: FROM CONCEPT TO IMPLEMENTATION

Maria Rodriguez, a Scrum Master for a mid-size fintech firm, gazed at the screen of her laptop on Monday morning with a sense of overwhelm at the number of possibilities she'd discovered about AI-facilitated Agile practices. She'd heard of sentiment analysis in retrospectives, backlog prioritization using AI, and smart sprint planning; but where exactly did she start? Her team was already having trouble adopting basic Agile, and introducing AI complexity seemed too daunting an endeavour.

What Maria required was not more theory; she required ready-to-apply practical tools and templates to assist her in making the first tangible steps toward AI-fortified Agile techniques. She required a starter package that would walk her team through their journey of transformation without burying them under complexity.

This chapter delivers exactly that: a complete set of tools, templates, checklists, and resources to help you apply AI-fortified Agile practices in your organization. If you're a Scrum Master such as Maria, a Product Owner wanting to enhance backlog management, or an Agile Coach facilitating organizational change, you'll find practical resources to speed up your way.

The AI-Agile Implementation Framework

Before getting into particular tools, know the background framework that successful AI-Agile adoption lies on:

Start Simple: Start with simple AI augmentations to existing Agile practices instead of trying full-scale transformation.

Focus on Value: Select AI applications that most directly alleviate team pain points or strongly enhance current processes.

Maintain Human Agency: Have AI enhance instead of displace human decision-making and collaboration.

Build Incrementally: Implement AI capabilities incrementally, so that teams can accommodate and learn before bringing in further complexity.

Measure Impact: Measure both quantitative data and qualitative feedback to know how well AI improvements are working.

Essential Templates and Tools

1. AI-Enhanced User Story Template

Classic user stories are all about functional requirements. AI-enriched user stories include added considerations for smart features:

As a [user type],

I want [functionality]

So that [business value]

AI Considerations:

- Data Requirements: What information is required for AI capability?
- Explainability: How will users comprehend AI choices?
- Bias Mitigation: What measures provide fairness to all user groups?
- Fallback Behavior: What occurs when AI systems do not work?
- Privacy Protection: How is user information safeguarded?

Acceptance Criteria:

[Conventional criteria]

- AI system provides explanations in clear language
- Bias testing done across applicable demographic segments

- Fallback mechanisms tested and documented
- Privacy impact assessment done

2. Sprint Planning Intelligence Checklist

This checklist assists teams in integrating AI insights into sprint planning while ensuring collective decision-making:

Pre-Planning Preparation:

- AI backlog analysis is complete (priority recommendations, complexity estimates)
- Team capacity forecast is generated (historical velocity, planned time off, external dependencies)
- Risk assessment is complete (technical debt, external dependencies, skill gaps)
- Customer feedback synthesis is available (sentiment analysis, feature usage statistics)

During Planning:

- Human-reasoned suggestions offered together with AI advice
- Team validates and discusses AI suggestions
- AI projections and team feedback taken into account during capacity allocation
- Risk of dependencies recognized and mitigation plans established
- Sprint objective is aligned with both business goals and technical limitations

Post-Planning:

- Commitments by the sprint noted with confidence intervals
- AI-recommended features with success criteria defined
- Experimental work learning objectives identified
- Mechanisms of feedback set up for improvement in AI system

3. Retrospective Insight Dashboard Template

The template frames retrospective discussions in terms of AI-derived insights while maintaining the human aspects that enable retrospectives to be useful:

Quantitative Insights (AI-Generated):

- Trends in team communication sentiment
- Team members' participation patterns
- Cycle time and flow efficiency measures
- Identification of repeating themes from past retrospectives

Qualitative Discussion Points:

- What are the patterns we observe in the AI insights?
- Where do our experiences vary from what is observed by the data?
- What context could the AI lack?

- How do we apply these insights to enhance our collaboration?

Action Planning:

- Specific, measurable changes based on both AI and human insights
- Tasks with clear ownership and deadlines
- Success criteria for measuring improvement effectiveness
- Plan to review progress in subsequent retrospectives

4. Acceptance Criteria for Responsible AI Story

This template integrates ethical principles into each AI-related user story:

Fairness and Bias:

- Model performance checked against relevant demographics
- Bias measurements calculated and recorded
- Strategies put in place to mitigate disparities found
- Periodic monitoring in place to continuously detect bias

Transparency and Explainability:

- Users able to comprehend how AI influences them
- Model limitations obviously explained

- Overriding or appeal processes in place when necessary
- Decision audit trails are kept for record-keeping

Privacy and Security:

- Data minimization guidelines followed
- User consent provided for data processing
- Data retention policies set and enforced
- Security appropriate for sensitivity level

Human Oversight:

- Apparent escalation routes for AI system failure
- Human review processes established for high-stakes decisions
- Override capabilities enabled for proper users
- Ongoing human verification of AI system behaviour

Implementation Roadmaps

90-Day Quick Start Plan

Days 1-30: Building the Foundation

- Evaluate existing Agile maturity utilizing supplied assessment template
- Determine 2-3 high-impact, low-risk AI improvement opportunities
- Define baseline metrics for chosen areas of improvement

- Initiate team training on AI basics and ethical AI practices

Days 31-60: Pilot Implementation

- Deploy first AI upgrade (suggested: retrospective sentiment analysis)
- Utilize supplied templates to organize AI-augmented ceremonies
- Gather feedback through organized assessment forms
- Tighten processes according to early learnings

Days 61-90: Scale and Refine

- Introduce second AI upgrade based on pilot learnings
- Train more team members in AI-Agile practices
- Start to measure impact using supplied metrics framework
- Schedule next phase of roll-out dependent on outcomes

Tool Selection Matrix

Selecting the appropriate tools is key to effective AI-Agile implementation. This matrix assists teams in making comparisons:

Measurement and Success Criteria Templates

Team Performance Metrics:

- Sprint velocity trends (pre- and post-AI deployment)
- Story completion percentage and spillover rate
- Team satisfaction ratings
- Ceremony time spent (efficiency improvements)
- Quality indicators (defect rates, rework rate)

AI System Performance Metrics:

- AI recommendation accuracy (acceptance rate of suggestions by teams)
- Satisfaction of users with AI tools
- Time gained via AI automation
- Quality of AI-created insights (usefulness ratings)
- Bias and fairness measures for AI systems

Business Impact Metrics:

- Reductions in time to market
- Customer satisfaction score increases
- Employee engagement increases
- Savings in cost due to process optimization
- Innovation metrics (new ideas created, experiments run)

Common Implementation Challenges and Solutions

Challenge: Team Resistance to AI Tools

Solutions: Begin with opt-in pilots, demonstrate clear value up front, and have human oversight over all decisions.

Challenge: AI Recommendations Don't Match Team Experience

Solutions: Utilize AI insights as discussion points instead of imperatives, and regularly tweak AI systems according to team input.

Challenge: Integration Complexity with Existing Tools

Solutions: Start with tools that incorporate smoothly with existing workflows without forcing significant platform upgrades at the outset.

Challenge: Measuring AI Impact

Solution: Measure baseline data prior to implementation and employ quantitative and qualitative metrics for measuring success.

Getting Started Action Plan

1. **Assessment:** Take the AI-Agile maturity assessment for your team

2. **Education:** Hold team workshops on AI basics and responsible AI behaviors

3. **Selection**: Select your first AI improvement using the decision matrix

4. Implementation: Utilize supplied templates to execute your initial AI-enhanced ceremony

5. Measurement: Create metrics and feedback collection mechanisms

6. Iteration: Revisit your methodology based on learnings and scale incrementally

Resource Library

Educational Resources:

- AI for Agile Teams: Fundamentals course outline
- Responsible AI practices checklist
- Team readiness assessment questionnaire
- Change management guidance for AI adoption

Technical Resources:

- API integration guides for widely used Agile tools
- Configuration templates for standard AI platforms
- Data privacy and security guidelines
- Troubleshooting guides for common issues

Key Takeaways

Good intentions are not enough to create successful AI-Agile implementation; practical tools, organized methods, and meticulous attention to technical and human factors are needed. The templates and resources in this chapter lay the groundwork for your start, but keep in mind that every team's path will be different.

The principle is to begin small, monitor effect, and iterate on learnings. Utilize these tools as a starting point, but be willing to tailor them to your team's context and needs. Most of all, keep human nature at the forefront of Agile use while employing AI to augment and augment human collaboration and decision-making.

In the next chapter, we will discuss how to measure your organization's AI-Agile maturity and develop a roadmap for scaling successful practices throughout your organization.

Chapter 13: The Maturity Map – Crawl, Walk, Run, Run, Fly Toward AI-Driven Agility

13

THE MATURITY MAP

FROM THE FIRST STEPS TO FULL-SCALE AI AGILITY

INTRODUCTION: THE JOURNEY, NOT THE END

Two teams at GlobalTech Solutions' headquarters in Austin were in conference rooms next to each other, and both said they had "successfully implemented AI in their Agile processes." Team Alpha was thrilled to show off their new AI-powered backlog prioritisation tool, which cut sprint planning time by 20%. Team Beta showed off their advanced AI ecosystem, which included autonomous agents who took care of regular development activities, predictive analytics that helped make strategic decisions, and machine learning models that constantly improved team performance based on feedback from the present.

Both teams were right: they had successfully included AI to their Agile methods. But they were at very different levels of development, with different skills, risks, and paths to progress. Leaders that are planning their organization's AI-

Agile transformation path need to know about these differences.

The hard part isn't figuring out if a company is "doing AI-Agile right." It's figuring out where they are on their maturity journey and what they need to do next. This chapter talks about a complete maturity framework that helps businesses figure out where they are now, plan how they will change, and stay away from frequent mistakes that might slow down AI-Agile changes.

The Four Stages of AI-Agile Maturity

Our maturity model is based on the "Crawl-Walk-Run-Fly" continuum, where each stage has its own set of skills, problems, and chances. Organisations can be at multiple maturity levels on several aspects at the same time, unlike linear development models.

Stage 1: Crawl—Looking Around and Trying Things Out

Companies at the Crawl stage are only starting to look into how AI could make their Agile methods better. Curiosity, exploration, and learning-focused projects are what make them special.

Key Features: -

AI experiments that happen on the fly inside each team

- Team members have a basic idea of what AI can do

- Traditional Agile ceremonies with only a little bit of AI added
- Not much control or standardisation of how AI is used
- More emphasis on learning than on scaling

Typical Activities:

- Pilot projects that use AI tools that are easy to find, such GitHub Copilot and Jira AI features.
- Workshops on the basics of AI and how to use it responsibly
- Teams discussing the results of their AI experiments in a casual way
- A simple evaluation of AI readiness and possible use cases

Common Problems:

- Not knowing where to start or what tools to use
- Team members and leaders not being familiar with AI
- Worrying about losing jobs and disrupting workflows
- Not being able to measure AI's impact and value

Success Indicators:

- Teams trying out AI tools on their own
- More interest in and learning about what AI can do

- Early success stories that get people want to learn more
- More people being aware of how to use AI responsibly

Example from the Real World: A developer at a medium-sized software company found GitHub Copilot and told his coworkers about it, which started their AI-Agile journey. In just a few months, three teams were trying out different AI coding helpers. The company also started holding monthly "AI Show and Tell" events where teams could talk about what they had learnt and tried.

Stage 2: Walk—Putting into practice and making everything the same

Organisations at the walk stage have gone beyond testing AI and are now using it on purpose in some Agile settings. They're starting to set standards and best practices while getting more teams to use AI.

Main Features:

- AI integration into several Agile rituals in a structured way
- New guidelines for choosing and using AI tools
- Basic responsible AI practices and governance
- Sharing AI across teams- improved Agile patterns
- First look into how AI affects team performance

Common Activities:

- AI-enhanced retrospectives that use sentiment analysis
- Predictive analytics help with sprint planning
- Standardised criteria for evaluating AI tools
- Making AI- Communities of practice that are agile
- Basic mechanisms for checking prejudice and fairness

Common Problems:

- Different teams use AI in different ways
- It's hard to make AI tools work with existing workflows
- Team members who are used to established methods are resistant to change.
- There aren't enough thorough governance frameworks.

Signs of Success:

- Different teams are effectively adopting AI-enhanced Agile methods
- Written down improvements in team performance metrics
- Set up ways to test and use new AI tools
- More faith in working with AI and people

Focus on Implementation: Companies should focus on creating repeatable patterns for AI-Agile integration, setting up basic governance frameworks, and gaining internal expertise through hands-on experience.

Stage 3: Run—Scaling and Improving

Organisations at the run stage have effectively spread AI-enhanced Agile processes across many teams and are improving their methods based on what they have learnt and the data they have collected.

Key Characteristics:

- Most development teams use AI-Agile techniques.
- Full governance frameworks and AI algorithms that are accountable
- Better integration between AI systems and Agile toolchains
- Using data to make AI better-improved processes
- AI-Agile projects that have a measurable effect on business

Common Tasks:

- AI across the whole company-Operations for the agile transformation office
- Advanced AI tools like automated testing and predictive capacity planning
- Programs for measuring bias and improving fairness in a thorough way
- AI that works across departments
- Agile teams made up of data scientists, ethicists, and specialists in the field

- Regularly checking and improving the performance of AI systems

Common Problems:

- Dealing with the complexity of AI systems that are linked together
- Making sure that quality and reliability stay the same across all implementations
- Finding a balance between standardisation and letting teams be creative and independent
- Keeping people's ability to make decisions and have control over their own lives

Success Indicators:

- AI's delivery has been getting better all the time-teams that are better
- Strong governance processes that stop problems with ethics and bias
- AI shows a strong return on investment-Investments that are agile
- Internal knowledge that can make unique AI solutions

Strategic Focus: Organisations should focus on sustainable growth, advanced governance, and continual optimisation as they become ready for more advanced AI applications.

Stage 4: Fly—Coming up with new ideas and changing things

Organisations that are at the fly stage are at the bleeding edge of AI-Agile integration. In these organisations, AI systems and human teams work together perfectly to achieve results that neither could achieve on their own.

Key Characteristics:

- AI systems are a big part of how organisations work and make decisions.
- AI agents that work on their own to do routine Agile tasks with human supervision
- AI systems and human processes that learn and adapt all the time
- Advanced applications like predicting organisational health and autonomous sprint optimisation
- Leadership in creating new AI- Patterns and practices that are agile

Common Activities:

- AI-powered digital twins for modelling how well a team or organisation does
- Self-directed sprint planning and retrospective facilitation with human oversight
- Advanced predictive analytics for strategic planning and risk management
- Cross-organizational AI-Working together in an agile way and sharing information
- Researching and developing AI-Agile capabilities for the next generation

Examples of Innovation:

- AI systems that can predict and stop team burnout before it happens
- Autonomous agents that help teams work together to solve problems
- Machine learning models that make the organisation more flexible by improving its structure
- AI-powered simulation environments for testing changes to the organisation

Responsibilities of a Leader

Organisations that are in the fly stage typically become thought leaders in the AI-Agile field, sharing their experience with others and helping to set industry standards.

Assessment of Multidimensional Maturity

Organisations seldom advance consistently across all facets of AI-Agile maturity. Our maturity evaluation framework looks at five important areas of maturity:

Technical Integration

- How advanced and integrated the tools are - How well you can build your own AI
- Infrastructure that is mature and can grow
- The quality and availability of data

Maturity of the Process

- Making AI-enhanced Agile processes the same across the board
- How advanced the governance system is - How good the change management is
- Processes for measuring and improving

Human Capital - AI literacy throughout the company - Specialised AI- Knowledge of Agile methods - The capacity to react to change and be ready for it - The ability to lead AI projects-Change to an agile way of working

AI that is ethical and responsible

- The ability to find and fix bias
- Practices for being open and clear
- Protecting privacy and managing data - Processes for considering the effects on stakeholders

Effect on Business

- Improvements in performance that can be measured
- Strategic edge from AI-Agile features
- New ideas and ways to stand out from the competition
- Making value that lasts

Strategies for Maturity Progression

From Crawl to Walk: - Work on making sure that all teams have a basic understanding of AI - Set up fundamental rules for governance and ethics

- Create patterns that AI can use over and over again- better ceremonies - make groups of people who share knowledge

From Walk to Run:

- Put money into training and skill building that covers everything - Set up governance and standards across the whole company
- Create AI solutions that are specific to the needs of the organisation
- Set up metrics and ways to make things better

From Run to Fly:

- Encourage new ideas and trying out new AI tools
- Make strategic collaborations with AI research groups
- Help the industry learn more and build best practices - Get ready for the next generation of AI capabilities and uses

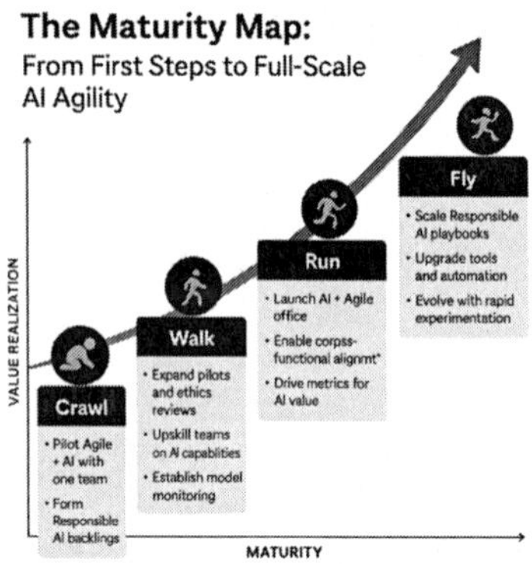

Common Maturity Mistakes and How to Avoid Them

Not going through all the steps: Companies that try to skip straight to advanced AI applications without first building up their basic skills generally fail, which slows down their whole transformation.

Solution: Follow the maturity progression and build skills in a planned way.

Technology-First Approach: If you only focus on AI tools and don't work on improving people's skills and getting the organisation ready, they won't be used much and won't have much of an effect.

Solution: Find a balance between using technology and developing people and managing change.

Governance Gaps: Without the right governance structures, scaling AI systems can lead to ethical problems and compliance challenges.

Solution: Build governance skills at the same time as technological skills.

Measurement Blindness: If you don't set clear goals for AI-Agile success, you can't improve your methods or show how valuable they are.

Solution: Use full measurement frameworks from the beginning of maturity growth.

Using the Maturity Model to Plan for Change

Process of Assessment:

1. Look at how mature each of the five dimensions is right now.

2. Find any gaps or irregularities between the dimensions.

3. Based on the aims and limits of the organisation, set realistic target maturity levels.

4. Make clear plans on how to improve your skills

5. Set goals and performance criteria for each maturity transition

Always Getting Better:

- Regular evaluations of maturity to see how things are going
- Changing methods based on what you've learnt and how things are changing
- Sharing what you've learnt with people inside and outside of your company - Getting ready for the next level of skills and problems

Important Points

AI-Agile maturity is not a goal to accomplish, but a process of learning and building skills that never ends. To be successful, you need to know where you are now, plan the right next actions, and grow your skills step by step instead of trying to jump forward to the next level.

The most successful organisations see maturity development as a constant process of trying new things, learning, and changing. They find a balance between ambition and realism, innovation and governance, and technological progress and human progress.

Maturity isn't just about using more advanced AI tools; it's also about building the skills and knowledge needed to utilise AI in a way that is responsible and helpful to people.

The AI-Agile maturity journey for your organisation is different from others, but the ideas and frameworks in this chapter can help you go through it effectively. The most important thing is to start where you are, grow up over time, and always remember the human needs that AI should meet.

In the last chapter, we'll talk about the leadership mentality and behaviours that make AI-Agile transformation work at any level of maturity.

Chapter 14: The Mindset Shift – Leading Mlindset Agile iin the Age of Intelligent Systems

14

LEADING THE FUTURE

THE AI-AGILE LEADER'S MINDSET

INTRODUCTION: THE PARADOX OF LEADERSHIP

At a packed Singapore convention center auditorium, Priya Chen, CTO at an international online shopping destination, was given her greatest leadership challenge to date. Her team had just demonstrated the mind-bending power of their AI-based recommendation platform for predicting customer palates with 94% accuracy. Bottom-line impacts were not ambiguous—conversion rates increased by 31%, customer satisfaction rankings hit record highs.

But then, in the demo, one of the team members asked a very bizarre question: "The AI is working fantastically for metros 25 to 45 years of age. What about people living in villages and above 50 years? Are we inherently creating a system where we are biased against some customers and biased against others?"

Priya saw at this time the essence of AI-Agile leadership: the very technologies that make us more effective and data-led press us to be more thoughtful, more cooperative, and more human in our decision-making. AI-facilitated Agile leadership is not about domesticating technology—it is about navigating the messy intersection of human values, technological capability, and organizational aspiration.

This chapter is on the mindsets, behaviors, and values on which leadership greatness in an AI-Agile-world depends, where the most important decisions are not technical but deeply human.

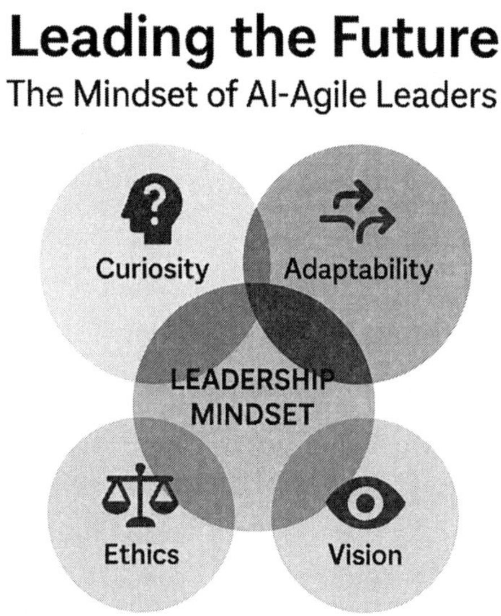

The Future of Leadership in the AI-Agile Age

The traditional models of leadership elegantly forecast linear cause-and effect between effort and outcome, neatly stated decision pyramids, and fairly predictable operating environments. But AI-Agile leadership faces a much different reality:

Exponential Change: The capability of AI increases exponentially, not step-wise, and thus leaders have to be capable of seeing accelerating, not step-wise, change.

Distributed Intelligence: Because AI systems can make their own thousands of micro-decisions, leadership is moved from direct control to direction-setting, boundary-making, and value-setting.

Ethical Complexity: With every AI-powered process come concerns with fairness, transparency, and human agency that require moral thought as well as technical knowledge.

Global Interconnection: Technology-leveraging collaboration spaces allow for global teams that are world-in-mind, necessitating inclusive leadership practice and cultural awareness.

Continuous Learning: AI ecosystem leaders must acquire continuous learning and intellectual humility.

The Five Pillars of AI-Agile Leadership

1. Curiosity Over Certainty

Leadership conventionally evokes self-confidence and definitiveness. AI-Agile leadership demands a reversal of intellectual curiosity and comfort with ambiguity.

Leap of Faith: AI technologies have the potential to make breathtaking insights and surprising patterns. Leadership that needs known solutions will be denied the lost advantage of the AI-enabled Agile practice transformation.

Question-Driven Leadership: Instead of answers, AI-Agile leaders ask better questions: "What are we assuming?" "How could we be mistaken?" "What would success look like to all stakeholders?"

Experimental Mindset: The mindset should be experimentation-led and exampled by leaders from learning through unforeseen consequences, embracing smart failures. That involves creating psychological safety so teams can experiment with risk-managed trials of AI implementations.

Life Example: When Satya Nadella became the CEO of Microsoft, he changed the culture from "know-it-all" to "learn-it-all." It was a paradigm shift because Microsoft embarked on incorporating AI into their product line, and top executives had to reboot what was possible on a day-to-day basis.

2. Systems Thinking in Complex Environments

AI and Agile leaders must recognize that changes in any aspect of the system will have lasting, often unforeseen, effects across the company and even across the company.

Interconnected Impact: Minor AI adjustment in appearance one presents can instill thoughts that will usher in innovation in product strategy, customer experience, and organizational objectives.

Leaders must see a feeling of prescience and anticipate ripple effects.

Stakeholder Ecosystem Sensitivity: AI technology is not an island—AI has effects on customers, employees, partners, and communities. Leaders will need to consider the entire stakeholder ecosystem in making AI decisions.

Long-term Impact Consideration: While Agile is a question of iteration in the short term, AI technology has long-term learning implications. Leaders need to balance short-term worth delivery against long-term system considerations.

Case Study: The AI-powered inventory optimization system of a retail company first delivered fantastic cost reductions. But the senior leadership soon discovered that the AI was optimizing short-term profitability at the cost of both supplier relationships and employee participation. They redesigned the system to optimize all stakeholders' outcomes and achieved improved long-term results.

3. Ethical Courage in AI Implementation

Most precious of AI-Agile leadership is the autonomy to take tough ethical decisions, especially if they disagree with maximizing short-term performance.

Values-Based Decision Making: In situations where AI results contradict organizational values or the greater good, leaders must be comfortable sacrificing short-term success for long-term integrity.

Preventive Bias Strategy: Rather than respond after issues of bias are uncovered, good leaders actively put in place procedures and systems that will identify and prevent imminent issues of fairness.

Transparent Communication: When AI does err or is biased in its results, good leaders communicate clearly to stakeholders what did happen, why it happened, and how it will not happen again in the future.

Stakeholder Advocacy: AI-Agile leaders must advocate for stakeholders who would otherwise not be heard by the development process—future clients, marginalized groups, or those which can be harmed by AI systems.

Business Problem: One of the financial service companies developed an automated procedure that considerably reduced loan approval time. The procedure was discriminatory against some parts of society, however, as auditors eventually discovered. The company's administration had to deploy the system with the flaws in trying to respond to competitive pressures, but held off deployment to resolve the bias issues and went ahead to develop a less biased and better system.

4. Servant Leadership for AI-Human Synergy

AI-Agile leadership is a revolutionary transformation from command-and-control to servant leadership in which the leader's primary duty is to facilitate others to succeed.

Enabling Human-AI Teams: Rather than delegating all AI decision-making to the middle, servant leaders enable teams to experiment with AI tools and create their own AI-human collaboration model.

Enabling AI Adoption: It involves providing training, infrastructure, and psychological safety to teams to try out AI augmentation of their Agile processes.

Enabling Cross-Functional Collaboration: AI deployment demands coordination between traditionally siloed functions—data science, engineering, product management, ethics, and law. Servant leaders set up structures and incentives where such collaboration can naturally happen and yield results.

Facilitating Continuous Learning: In the background of continuously growing AI powers, servant leaders are investing in facilitating their people continuous learning and adaptability abilities.

Implementation Example: The leadership of a software development firm changed the role of their department from a project management function to one of empowering teams. Instead of tracking adoption rates on multiple teams, now they needed to create obstacles, provide resources, and share good AI-Agile concepts from team to team, thereby making AI adoption more natural and sustainable.

5. Adaptive Resilience in Uncertain Environments

AI-Agile leaders must be resilient yet adaptable at the same time—providing steady guidance while quickly responding to new information. and changing situations.

Strategic Resilience with Tactical Adaptability: Leaders are rigidly committed to values and strategy vision but adaptable to implementation plans and short-term strategies.

Learning-Oriented Failure Response: With failure or surprise by means of AI systems, good leaders emphasize learning and improvement over blame and risk aversion.

Anticipatory Adaptation: Rather than adapting to change that provokes adaptation, anticipatory visionaries are perpetually looking for future trends and preparing their organizations for many different potential futures.

Emotional Regulation: Implementing AI instills fear and resistance within people and organizations. Leaders who are strong exercise emotional regulation and herding people through the psychological peaks and valleys of collaborating with AI.

Leading Through AI-Agile Transformation

Creating Psychological Safety for AI Experimentation

AI-Agile leaders must create spaces where the teams have liberty to experiment and try out AI tools, raise concerns freely without apprehension, and override AI recommendations whenever they are in conflict with human judgment or ethics.

Modeling Vulnerability: Leaders who make themselves vulnerable for other people to understand that even them have an AI learning curve and that they ask for assistance from other people provide other people a license to be learners and not experts.

Intelligent Failure Celebrations: Leaders celebrate failure in AI testing as learnings and not as failure.

Skeptical Mindset: Leaders must award and recognize employees who are skeptical of AI recommendations and make counterarguments based on human intuition and experience.

AI-Literate Organizations

Learning Commitment: AI-Agile leaders have to learn continuously about what AI can do and what it cannot, and how it impacts everything.

Investing in Team Development: Beyond technical AI training, but responsible AI practices, bias detection, and human-AI collaboration skills.

Developing Communities of Practice: Learning can be enabled by bringing people within the company together who have the same pain points with AI-Agile.

Establishing External Networks: Converse with industry communities, academic researchers, and other professionals to get new best practices.

Scaling AI-Agile Practices Responsibly

Phased Rollout: Rather than upgrading AI in all locations simultaneously, senior leaders first pilot projects, track results, and phase-forward successful pilots.

Cultural Reinforcement: Designing AI updates that reinforce and augment organisational culture rather than dismantling human relationships and collaboration.

Monitoring and Tensioning: Ongoing monitoring of outcomes on performance and human impact, with strategy tweaks as a result of learning and changing conditions.

Long-term Sustainability: Building AI-Agile capabilities able to learn and adapt to technological and organisational change.

The Personal Leadership Journey

Self-Assessment for Leaders

Effective AI-Agile leaders consistently assess their own strengths and weaknesses:

- **Technical Acumen:** Do I possess an adequate grasp of the strengths and weaknesses of AI to make effective decisions?
- **Moral Decision Making**: Can I make difficult moral decisions when AI systems present ethical challenges?
- **Change Leadership:** Am I guiding others with fear and awe of collaboration with AI?
- **Systems Perspective**: Am I thinking in terms of the ecosystem of how projects that involve AI will impact things?
- **Learning Agility**: Am I constantly updating what I know as AI capability grows?

Building Your Leadership Platform

Vision Development: Establish a solid vision for how human intelligence and AI can collaborate to generate value for all stakeholders.

Stakeholder Engagement: Engage different stakeholders—technologists, ethicists, customers, and citizens of society—to construct your leadership plan.

Influence Building: Enhance your influencing ability by using narrative power, evidence-based reasoning, and values-based reasoning.

Networking Cultivation: Connect with other AI-Agile leaders to share experiences and learn from different perspectives.

The Legacy of AI-Agile Leadership

The pioneering AI-Agile leaders will not be celebrated for having exploited the technology, but for having united people and smart systems and generated value, resolved problems, and improved lives.

They will have:

- Upheld human agency and dignity while reaping the benefits of AI capabilities
- Built more equitable and just organizations through the adoption of AI on principle
- Built adaptive capacities that serve their companies beautifully beyond the span of time in which technology granted expires

- Exhibited value-led decision-making that renders individuals satisfied with value congruence with performance
- Embracing culture of lifelong learning and ethical innovation

Key Takeaways

Effective leadership in the AI-Agile age will require a new head and a new leadership style. It will not anymore be technology-driven but by the abilities to overcome sophisticated human-technology interfaces with wisdom, bravery, and humility.

The most essential leadership skills are actually human: empathy, moral leadership, systems thinking, and inspiring people to do their best work alongside intelligent machines.

Remember, as you develop your own AI-Agile leadership model, your greatest responsibility isn't the technology itself, but the individuals whose work and lives will be affected by how it will be utilized and implemented.

The future requires leaders to unleash the power of AI without losing and sacrificing what makes us beautifully human. It's not if you're prepared to lead in the AI-Agile era—it's if you're prepared to empower others to thrive in it.

It begins with one promise: to lead with heart and mind, leveraging AI to augment human potential, not replace it, and building organizations that work for all stakeholders, not just the technologically enabled privileged few.

Your responsibility to make that a reality is larger than you could ever have imagined. Your decisions, the culture we create, and values we instill will determine what occurs for generations to come at the intersection of human and artificial intelligence. Make your decisions count.

THE PATH FORWARD -
DESIGNIG THE
DESIGNIG THE
FUTURE OF
WIF WORK
WITH AI-POWERED
AGILITY

CONCLUSION

THE NEXT STEP

As we conclude our journey to the intersection of artificial intelligence and Agile methodologies, it's worth considering how far we've traveled; not merely through the pages of this book, but as a profession, as an industry, and as individuals who are learning to adapt to a rapidly changing world of work.

The individuals who penned the Agile Manifesto in 2001 could not have imagined that AI would ever assist humans to develop software. They were more concerned about people and interactions than about technology and processes. Yet they likely did not know that among some of those "people" could be AI copilots capable of writing code, sentiment reading, and estimating how a project will turn out. But the most important qualities they discussed; collaboration, flexibility, customer focus, and receptiveness to change; are still essential and even more so now that AI exists. We are at a similar point in time now.

The combination of AI and Agile is more than a shift in technology; it's an entirely new way of thinking about how humans and intelligent systems can collaborate to make things better, solve hard problems, and create higher-quality goods and services. This change is already occurring, not whether it will occur. The question is whether we will guide it in a way that is open, moral, and well thought out. The Change We've Seen This book talks about how AI is affecting every area of Agile practice:

In our ceremonies, we've seen daily stand-ups evolve from reporting on the project's progress to sessions where people work together to come up with new ideas.

This is due to the fact that AI considers the way team members communicate with each other and the progress of the project.

AI currently suggests sprint planning based on facts, but people can still use their own judgment and imagination. Sentiment analysis and pattern detection have made retrospectives more significant by making it possible for teams to discover ways to improve that they might not otherwise have considered. We've witnessed the emergence of AI copilots enhancing human abilities rather than replacing them in our careers.

Scrum Masters are able to notice things regarding how the team collaborate and likely issues nobody else can.

Product Owners discover what customers desire and how to utilize data to determine which features are most essential

AI assistants enable developers to code more efficiently and faster with better code while ensuring security and quality regulations.

In our organizations, we've explored how transformation offices are evolving to facilitate greater collaboration between AI and Agile on a large scale. This ensures that ethical concerns and proper AI practices are considered right from the beginning rather than being brought in later. We've witnessed how AI has improved Agile principles and how they're transforming supply chain management, manufacturing, robotics, and even decentralised autonomous businesses. This is more than just writing software in the traditional manner. Companies are discovering new ways to generate new ideas by blending iterative development with clever automation.

The Good and Bad Things That Will Happen

As we look to the future, the theoretical benefits of AI-enhanced Agile methodologies are huge:

Democratised Intelligence: AI technology is making it simple for teams of any size and technical expertise to leverage powerful analytical tools. Now even small businesses can tap into the same types of clever automation and forecasting tools that only big corporations with their own data science teams could formerly afford.

Worldwide Inclusion: AI tools such as BharatGen that are capable of operating in more than one language are eradicating language barriers and making it possible for people from all over the world to collaborate.

All team members can communicate in their own native language and yet comprehend one another and work toward the same objective.

Enhanced Human Capabilities: AI does not deprive us of our judgement and creativity; it improves us by automating dull mental tasks so that we can concentrate on strategic thinking, innovative problem-solving, and collaboration in a productive manner.

Continuous Learning: AI systems that learn from the way teams work and how projects turn out form improvement loops that continually make the teams and the AI systems better. This is referred to as a cycle of improvement.

Yet we must beware the great responsibilities and potential risks associated with these promises:

The Danger of Dehumanisation:

It's simpler to allow computers to make decisions on behalf of people and simplify tough conditions as AI becomes more intelligent.

The tough part is harnessing AI's analytical capabilities but also maintaining the human elements that make Agile function, like empathy, creativity, and ethical thinking.

Bias and Fairness: AI systems trained on past data might retain and even exacerbate present biases, potentially making teamwork less inclusive rather than more. Being mindful of bias and fairness at all times is imperative.

Privacy and Autonomy: The more effective AI systems become at observing how teams collaborate and behave, we must find a reasonable balance between collecting valuable information and protecting individuals' privacy and mental well-being.

The Control of Talent: AI skills might end up in the possession of large technology firms or moneyed groups who may render it more difficult for teams and organisations to compete and generate new ideas.

Rules for the Future

We should adopt a few important rules as we navigate this transition:

Human-Centered AI: Technology must assist people in flourishing and succeeding, and not the reverse. All AI advancements to Agile processes must make work more purposeful, make collaboration more effective, and make results greater for all parties involved.

Ethical by Design: Responsible AI practices are not nice-to-haves; they must be part of how we use AI in Agile processes from the beginning. This will mean that every process empowered by AI begins with fairness, honesty, and accountability.

Inclusive Innovation: The advantages of AI-fortified Agile processes ought to translate across a broad variety of cultures, languages, and businesses. We must strive to prevent new digital divides from occurring.

Continuously learning: Both AI systems and man should constantly learn. Businesses must invest in educating their employees on how to use AI and ensure that AI systems continue to improve based on what actual people have to say and what they require.

Collaborative intellect: The future is not one in which AI surpasses human intelligence, but rather one in which we create new forms of collaborative intelligence where AI systems and humans collaborate to compensate for each other's strengths and weaknesses.

How You Can Help Make the Future Better

When you complete this book and return to the workplace, you will have thc opportunity; and the responsibility; to influence how this change occurs in your company and your sector.

What you do matters if you are a team member, a manager, or a beginner learning about AI-facilitated Agile processes.

Begin Where You Are: You don't need to wait until everything is perfect or until your business has a great start with lots of plans. Start with small experiments, learn from the outcome, and then slowly build up speed. You can use the tools and templates in this book as a good starting point, but you need to modify them to fit your needs and circumstances.

Lead with Values: As you use AI in your Agile work, make your values drive the decisions. Prioritize team psychological safety, customer benefit, and moral concerns at the top, combined with making things more efficient and better.

Stay Curious: AI is constantly evolving, and new things are always emerging. Stay open-minded, stay connected with other individuals who do the same thing you do, and be willing to change the way that you do it as you continue to learn and improve at doing it.

Build Bridges: Demonstrate to your colleagues the advantages and disadvantages of using AI to enhance Agile processes. Blog what you've learned, assist new colleagues, and become part of the larger community of experts.

Support Inclusion: Exercise your influence to ensure that AI-powered Agile methods benefit all, not only those who are already privileged.

Support creating tools and processes that accommodate multiple languages, are simple to operate, and are built to include everyone.

The Future We're Creating Together

It's not merely a shift in software development or running projects that AI and Agile are converging. It is part of a bigger movement in how individuals collaborate to address hard issues and improve things in an increasingly interconnected world.

We're collaborating to create a world in which AI manages routine analysis and coordination so that teams of people can concentrate on creative and strategic work. Collaboration on a global scale is really inclusive, as intelligent translation and cultural adaptation dissolve language and cultural barriers.

- Information and knowledge enable individuals to make improved choices yet remain rooted in their personal beliefs and judgment.
- Organisations can adapt faster and more intelligently yet not lose their stability and mission.
- Balancing human creativity with AI-enabled experimentation accelerates innovation.

The Journey Continues

This book is complete, but your journey is just beginning. The concepts, strategies, and principles we've discussed here will evolve as you apply them in your own life. The AI systems will get better, the Agile practices will evolve to face new challenges, and the two will work together more effectively.

The basic human needs that Agile practices respond to; like the need for purpose, teamwork, constant improvement, and meaningful work; will never change.

AI can assist us in fulfilling these needs more effectively, but it can't substitute for the people and common objectives that make superior teams excellent.

As you continue on your journey, remember that technology must serve people, not the reverse.

AI should assist humans in becoming better at what they do, not replace their capacity to decide.

Don't make things less fair and more closed by creating systems that do that.

Don't create ways that monitor and control individuals; instead, create ones that make teams safer and more efficient.

Today, individuals everywhere are writing the future of work in groups and businesses. You can assist in writing that story by ensuring it's one of people improving with the assistance of intelligent technology, collaborating across borders due to inclusive design, and continually improving according to moral principles. The road forward is tough, but it also holds fresh chance to improve our work, work more efficiently together, and develop new ideas.

AI and Agile complement each other perfectly to allow us to handle uncertainty, fix difficult problems, and create products and services that really meet people's needs. Today is the day to begin.

Begin small, think big, continue learning, and construct the future of work one sprint, one postmortem, and one human-AI relationship at a time.

The future is smart, flexible, and deeply human.

And it begins with you.

APPENDIX: ACTIONABLE TEMPLATES & TOOLKITS

1. **AI-Agile Role Augmentation Map**

Use this matrix to define how each Agile role (PO, SM, Dev, QA, Coach) can integrate AI Copilots and automation tools in their day-to-day workflows.

Agile Role	AI Capabilities to Leverage	Tools Suggested	Benefits Delivered
Product Owner	Smart prioritization, ROI forecasting	Aha!, ProductBoard	Data-driven decisions, faster delivery
Scrum Master	Mood tracking, blocker prediction	ScrumGenius, TeamRetro	Early impediment removal
Developer	AI code generation, intelligent test cases	GitHub Copilot, CodeWhisperer	Faster, secure coding
Agile Coach	Maturity dashboards, transformation metrics	Miro AI, Jira Align	Organization-wide improvement visibility

2. AI-Infused Sprint Planning Canvas

A guided template for teams to plan sprints using AI inputs.

Planning Item	Inputs from AI Copilot	Human Team Notes
Team Capacity	Forecasted load based on past sprints	Confirm leaves, blockers
Story Prioritization	Based on customer feedback + ROI analysis	PO confirms based on business needs
Risk & Dependency Alerts	Automated identification from code/repo/data	Dev + SM validate
Success Metrics Projection	AI predictions for sprint goals	Adjust based on stakeholder input

3. AI-Agile Maturity Assessment

Self-evaluation tool for organizations to assess their maturity in integrating AI into Agile practices.

Maturity Area	Criteria	Current State (1–5)	Action Items
AI Tool Adoption in Ceremonies	AI used in planning, retrospectives, reviews, standups		
Role Augmentation	Use of AI copilots across Agile roles		
Ethical AI Practices	Fairness, transparency, and responsible AI use in teams		
Cross-functional Collaboration	AI supporting cross-role workflows and decisions		
Continuous Learning Culture	Teams iterating AI feedback into practices		

4. AI-Augmented Ceremonies Toolkit

A toolkit to enhance Agile ceremonies with AI:

- Stand-ups: AI-generated summaries, sentiment trend alerts
- Sprint Planning: Velocity forecasts, smart prioritization engine
- Retrospectives: Sentiment and trend analysis, backlog improvement recommendations

- Reviews: Customer sentiment analytics, usage trend reports

🛠 Recommended Tools: Otter.ai + Jira, Confluence AI, Standuply, TeamRetro

5. Framework Selector for AI + Agile Projects

Decision table to select the right Agile framework based on team size, complexity, and AI focus.

Context	Suggested Framework	Why
Single-team AI model R&D	Kanban	Flexible with experimental uncertainty
Enterprise-scale AI initiative	SAFe	Alignment and governance across functions
Rapid feature delivery	Scrum	Iterative with defined feedback cycles
Efficiency + Automation Focus	Lean	Continuous improvement and waste reduction
Complex org setup	Hybrid (e.g., Scrumban + Lean)	Custom-fit agility with flow & optimization

6. AI Ethics & Bias Checklist for Agile Teams

Incorporate during backlog refinement and sprint reviews.

- ✅ Are fairness criteria defined in user stories?
- ✅ Was bias testing performed during model development?
- ✅ Was there a retrospective discussion on ethical implications?
- ✅ Are there explainability mechanisms built into the AI models?
- ✅ Was feedback from affected users considered in design?

7. AI Sprint Outcome Dashboard (Sample Format)

Capture key performance indicators from AI-augmented sprints.

Metric	Before AI	After AI Copilot Integration	Notes
Avg. Sprint Goal Completion	68%	84%	Based on TechFin example
Planning Time	4 hrs	2.5 hrs	Time saved with pre-analysis
Blocker Resolution Time	Avg. 3 days	Avg. 1.5 days	Sentiment and code repo analysis

8. Agile AI Learning Pathways

For practitioners to upskill based on roles.

Role	Learning Focus	Suggested Resources
Scrum Master	AI for trend analysis & team mood detection	Coursera NLP, TeamRetro guides
Product Owner	AI for ROI modeling & prioritization	DataCamp Product Analytics
Developer	Generative AI for coding	GitHub Copilot Labs, OpenAI APIs
Agile Coach	Organizational AI maturity, team metrics	SAFe DevOps + AI case studies

REFERENCES

Amazon Web Services. (n.d.). *Amazon CodeWhisperer*. https://aws.amazon.com/codewhisperer/

Atlassian. (2024). *Atlassian Intelligence for Jira and Confluence*. https://www.atlassian.com/solutions/ai

BharatGen Project. (n.d.). *BharatGen: India's open-source multilingual AI*. Retrieved from https://ai4bharat.org/ (or your actual project link if different)

Celonis. (n.d.). *Celonis process mining*. https://www.celonis.com/

DeepL. (n.d.). *DeepL API*. https://www.deepl.com/pro-api

GitHub. (2024). *GitHub Copilot*. https://github.com/features/copilot

GitLab. (2024). *GitLab 2024 Remote Work Report*. https://about.gitlab.com/remote-work-report/

Google. (2019). *Model cards for model reporting*. Google Research. https://arxiv.org/abs/1810.03993

IBM. (n.d.). *AI governance and ethics*. https://www.ibm.-com/artificial-intelligence/ai-ethics

Kinaxis. (n.d.). *RapidResponse platform*. https://www.ki-naxis.com/en/products/rapidresponse

Lexion. (n.d.). *AI-powered contract management*. https://www.lexion.ai/

Minit. (n.d.). *Minit process mining*. https://www.minit.io/

MLflow. (n.d.). *MLflow open source platform for the machine learning lifecycle*. https://mlflow.org/

o9 Solutions. (n.d.). *o9 AI-powered integrated business planning*. https://o9solutions.com/

OpenAI. (2024). *ChatGPT*. https://chat.openai.com/

Otter.ai. (n.d.). *AI meeting notes and transcription*. https://otter.ai/

Pactum. (n.d.). *AI contract negotiation*. https://www.-pactum.com/

Power BI. (n.d.). *Business analytics solutions*. Microsoft. https://powerbi.microsoft.com/

Tabnine. (n.d.). *AI code assistant*. https://www.tabnine.com/

Vernacular.ai. (n.d.). *AI-powered speech recognition for Indian languages*. https://vernacular.ai/

Vertex AI. (n.d.). *Vertex AI: Unified machine learning platform*. Google Cloud. https://cloud.google.com/vertex-ai

Additional references mentioned

- Beck, K., et al. (2001). *Manifesto for Agile software development*. https://agilemanifesto.org/
- Scaled Agile, Inc. (n.d.). *Scaled Agile Framework (SAFe)*. https://scaledagileframework.com/
- Scrum.org. (n.d.). *Scrum guide.* https://scrumguides.org/
- Google. (n.d.). *Google Cloud Translation API.* https://cloud.google.com/translate

lades, awards, and the trust of the global practitioner ecosystem.

"AI Meets Agile: Transforming the Way We Work" is more than his debut book—it's a culmination of years of field-work, leadership lessons, and bold thinking on the future of intelligent agility.

He continues to explore new frontiers at the intersection of human potential and machine intelligence—and is already working on the next installment in the series.

You can connect with him on LinkedIn: linkedin.com/in/vinaybabutarala

ABOUT THE AUTHOR

Vinay Babu Tarala is a global thought leader at the intersection of Agile transformation and AI-powered innovation. With over two decades of experience in digital product management, enterprise agility, and procurement technologies, he has helped Fortune 500 organizations navigate complexity and embrace change.

Vinay is known for his practical yet visionary approach to integrating emerging technologies into everyday work. As a PMI Pearl City Hyderabad chapter leader, international conference speaker, and Agile coach, he has empowered thousands of professionals across industries to adapt, evolve, and lead with purpose.

He has spoken at premier global forums including the PMI Global Summit, PMI Leadership Institute Meetings, and various Agile and AI conferences across Asia and beyond. His work spans enterprise AI integrations, agile transformation roadmaps, and coaching high-performing teams.

Vinay holds numerous industry certifications including PMP®, PMO-CP®, DASSM®, ICP-ACC®, and SAFe® Program Consultant. His contributions to the project management and Agile community have earned him acco-